SPECULATIVE
FUTURES

SPECULATIVE FUTURES

DESIGN APPROACHES TO NAVIGATE CHANGE, FOSTER RESILIENCE, AND CO-CREATE THE CITIES WE NEED

JOHANNA HOFFMAN

North Atlantic Books
Huichin, unceded Ohlone land
aka Berkeley, California

Published by
North Atlantic Books
Huichin, unceded Ohlone land
aka Berkeley, California

Cover art © ChaiwatUD via Shutterstock,
jakkaje879 via Shutterstock
Cover design by Emma Hall
Book design by Happenstance Type-O-Rama

Printed in Canada

Speculative Futures: Design Approaches to Navigate Change, Foster Resilience, and Co-create the Cities We Need is sponsored and published by North Atlantic Books, an educational nonprofit based in the unceded Ohlone land Huichin (*aka* Berkeley, CA) that collaborates with partners to develop cross-cultural perspectives, nurture holistic views of art, science, the humanities, and healing, and seed personal and global transformation by publishing work on the relationship of body, spirit, and nature.

North Atlantic Books' publications are distributed to the US trade and internationally by Penguin Random House Publisher Services. For further information, visit our website at www.northatlanticbooks.com.

Library of Congress Cataloging-in-Publication Data

Names: Hoffman, Johanna, 1986– author.
Title: Speculative futures : design approaches to navigate change, foster
    resilience, and co-create the cities we need / Johanna Hoffman.
Description: Berkeley, California : North Atlantic Books, [2022] | Includes
    bibliographical references and index. | Summary: "This dynamic field
    guide describes how speculative futures—design approaches used to
    visualize and respond to what lies ahead—can help us build more
    sustainable and equitable cities for everyone"—Provided by publisher.
Identifiers: LCCN 2022003547 | ISBN 9781623177362 (trade paperback) | ISBN
    9781623177379 (ebook)
Subjects: LCSH: City planning—Environmental aspects. | Cities and
    towns—Growth.
Classification: LCC HT166 .H634 2022 | DDC 307.1/216—dc23/eng/20220526
LC record available at https://lccn.loc.gov/2022003547

1 2 3 4 5 6 7 8 9 MARQUIS 27 26 25 24 23 22

This book includes recycled material and material from well-managed forests. North Atlantic Books is committed to the protection of our environment. We print on recycled paper whenever possible and partner with printers who strive to use environmentally responsible practices.

To Genevieve,
for always showing the way.

CONTENTS

We are what we imagine. Our very existence consists in our imagination of ourselves.

—N. SCOTT MOMADAY

Games are the prelude to serious ideas.

—CHARLES AND RAY EAMES

AUTHOR'S NOTE

LET ME START by stating the obvious—the title of this book is redundant. All visions of the future are speculative. To imagine what the future might be is to speculate about what has yet to, or may never, occur. So why adopt such a redundant expression? Why is speculative futures a phrase worth using?

One reason is entirely practical. Speculative futures is a widely employed umbrella term for the array of design approaches used to create high-resolution visions of potential realities. Science fiction is a form of speculative futures. The worldbuilding that shapes Marvel films is another. The range of tactics that provocatively explore what the future could become is what many call speculative futures.

More importantly, however, describing futures as speculative is a way of challenging the status quo. Ideally, our capacities to envision the future would be strong enough to see beyond the political division, climatic catastrophe, and economic inequality that dictate so much of the present. Yet that isn't the case.[1] Our ideas about the future are haunted by the logic of our pasts and hampered by the norms of the present. Insisting on futures as speculative tacitly reshapes that dynamic, inviting us to see the conceptual shackles we so often adopt, think differently about what could be, and actively engage in the project of collective self-creation. Naming futures as speculative is a means of reclaiming of how the future is shaped.

I'm hopeful that the term will soon become outdated, that our imaginative capacities will grow so strong that current circumstances will no longer limit our ideas of what is possible. For now, however, speculative futures has value, both as a name for tools to creatively envision alternative realities, and as a reminder that each of us has the ability to imagine and build the futures we want for this world.

A street view of a more watery San Francisco from an installation set in the year 2200 (2016).

INTRODUCTION

THE YEAR IS 2200. I'm standing in the living room of a seventh-floor San Francisco apartment, getting ready to go outside. A pair of waders hangs by the door, next to a canoe paddle for navigating the flooded streets outside. Air-filtration masks and a silver-coated coolsuit dangle from adjacent pegs. A note pinned next to the objects insists the suit isn't necessary—it's only 101°F outside. The filtration masks, however, are critical. Particulate levels are at 720 parts per million, high enough not just to poison my lungs but to slow my thoughts as well.

The living room was an art installation. I built it in 2016 for a San Francisco street festival, creating a space people could step inside as if they were renting it for the weekend. A bowl of dry shampoo sat on a table next to the couch. A note from the owner encouraged visitors to stay hydrated in the desert weather and enjoy the local tequila and saltwater potatoes. A sign signaled that the tap water was safe to drink but—with drought widespread and premium filtered bottles selling for as much as two hundred dollars—it came from treated wastewater.

I made the installation to explore two simple yet hard-to-confront truths: climate change is real, and seas are already rising. While we have little choice but to adapt, few cities provide space to reflect on what those changes mean for daily life. How will going to the doctor be different? What will I snack on in the middle of the day? When climate-changed seas have risen twenty-five feet, and coastal California temperatures regularly hit triple digits, are morning showers still a thing? Inviting people to interact with objects needed to navigate urban life in two hundred years was a way to translate climate change from abstract concept to lived experience.

Placed on a downtown sidewalk for three days, the installation became a site for debate on rates of sea-level rise, heat-wave frequencies, and ideas for how to respond. Some people sat inside for hours, watching the light shift on the apartment's false windows depicting the world outside: San Francisco as a twenty-third-century Venice.[1] Several cried. Many yelled.

The force of people's reactions surprised me. I thought a living room from the future would be a way to inject some lightness into the heavy conversations so often surrounding climate change. Trying on waterproof waders and handling canoe paddles in the middle of a busy street seemed playful. I hoped the process might elicit some deeper feelings, but I didn't expect the waves of intensity that arose. One woman snuffled into a tissue as she walked around the space, snapping "Step back!" at a fellow participant when he asked her if she was okay. Another man gripped my hand as he left, thanking me through tears.

There was something powerful, I began to realize, about having shared spaces to process our fears and start imagining previously unimaginable futures.

Building that living room from 2200 ushered me into a field I soon learned to call *speculative futures*. Design approaches that play with the space between fantasy and reality, speculative futures takes a range of forms. Writing science fiction is one kind. Creating physical objects from the future is another. Curious about the dark sides of science and technology, Mary Shelley wrote *Frankenstein* to explore what would happen if a young scientist fabricated a human being. Steven Spielberg made *Minority Report* to investigate the kind of world that would arrest people for crimes they've yet to commit. Regardless of strategy, speculative futures collapses the distance between tomorrow and today, creating experiences that help us reflect on the ramifications of potential change.

I was a traditional urban designer when I discovered the world of speculative futures. I spent my days grading parking garages, setting curb heights, and shaping playgrounds. While the tools I found in the speculative space were new to me, they had strong connections to those I used at work. Both fields operate largely in the imaginative realm, employing tactics to cultivate and refine creative thinking. Urban designers explore, articulate, and test potential visions before implementing anything in physical form. Prior to construction, a building often exists for years as an idea, in presentations, drawings, and diagrams. A city masterplan might be based on scientific research and detailed models, but it remains a fiction until development begins. That fictional space is a critical time to see where improvements can be made. Every design proposal submitted for assessment is speculation waiting to be made real.

Yet speculation in urban design cultivates imagination that some employ in mercenary ways. Inside the studio, speculation is a tool to envision, iterate, and refine a possible future. Outside, it can become a means to present that same future as inevitable. Because development is a serious process, involving large funds, extensive time spans, and long-term consequences, designers and planners often feel pressure to depict a proposal less as a possibility than a guarantee. Policymakers and developers are bombarded with such conflicting expectations that any veneer of certainty can quickly become a life raft. This emphasis on certainty tacitly encourages people to perpetuate the status quo. A future that resembles what already exists is an easier future to sell.

Diving into speculative futures highlighted problems I'd noticed in my profession for years. When developing ideas within the office, coworkers and I would value the imaginative space, sketching schemes on trace paper, brainstorming on walls, and building detailed test models. When presenting to clients or potential funders, we cased that imagination in logical arguments, intent on proving a given proposal as not just the *best* but the *only* choice. At outreach events, we filled walls with diagrams, site maps, and renderings to persuade people toward our point of view. The approach often worked. Yet just as frequently, no matter how many graphics we shared or how much food we brought, participants would grow disinterested, frustrated, or confused. After one workshop designed to explore what a semi-suburban enclave wanted to do about mounting heat wave risks, I approached a concerned-looking woman and asked her what was wrong. "I don't get what this means for me," she said. "I need to *feel* what you're talking about."

Sitting in that living room installation on that city street in 2016, I began to understand what the woman was saying. Unlike my previous projects, the art piece wasn't selling a vision of what life should be. It invited people into a version of what reality could become and asked them what they thought in response. With its waders and paddles and views of a watery San Francisco, the living room transformed a future of long-term climatic change into a process with intimate impact. Sensing what days could be like when the world is a warmer place helped visitors express the sadness, anger, and curiosity they felt as a result. It gave them room to explore and share what they wanted to see instead. By stepping into a potential future, people were able to access and discuss the feelings so many of us keep to ourselves—loss, fear, and hope about what could be.

Feeling into the future expands our imaginations of what cities can become. We need that expansion. Approaching city-making as a process with guaranteed results perpetuates the idea that the future can be forecasted and controlled. Given today's scales, scopes, and speeds of change, that kind of thinking is dangerous. Coming decades will only make it more so. Summer temperatures will continue to spike higher than existing cooling systems have been designed to handle. Internet access and storage demands are already outpacing available tools. Even with the best research and foresight, urban life will continue to morph in ways beyond prediction. The past is not a sufficient template for what lies ahead.

Limited imagination also extends urban development's long legacies of exclusion. For generations, the work of city-making has limited public participation to minimize opposition and accelerate built work.[2] Many communities have been dismissed, disenfranchised, and displaced as a result, setting the stage for many of the social and economic inequalities plaguing cities today. Aiming for approval over collaboration reinforces those exclusive patterns, prolonging the narrative that cities are spaces only experts can shape. When imagination is a means for persuasion in development, the benefits are rarely evenly distributed.[3]

Clinging to threads of certainty ultimately limits our imagination about what cities can become. Presenting futures as predictable requires grounding them in today's logic. Yet the confines of conventional wisdom often turn envisioning alternative trajectories into impossible tasks. Because environmental degradation is progressing at increasingly rapid rates, it's easy to assume total devastation is inevitable. Because exclusive planning is still the widespread norm, pushing for collaboration can feel impossible. Because privatization and deregulation have dominated Western societies for decades, many of us can't picture a future without them. Placing borders around our individual and collective imaginations makes long-standing issues appear increasingly intractable and dystopian futures more inevitable by the day.

By exploring what's possible, speculative futures cultivates critical thinking about the present and imagination of what lies ahead. The field embraces the fact that what we call "the future" is a construct, an amalgamation of assumptions, interpretations, and inferences based on experience, research, and hope. Rather than presenting ideas of where the future can go as certainties, speculative futures works with those constructs, employing dynamic tools for prototyping, testing, and evaluating the ramifications of where our imaginations can lead.

Celebrating the space between fantasy and reality builds the resilience this century requires. Studies show that actively imagining the future cultivates psychological strength, helping individuals feel more prepared and resourceful during times of drastic change.[4] Skill in envisioning potential futures increases our understanding of how present-day choices affect how futures unfold. Instead of craving extensions of the familiar, we can learn to find power in crafting proactive decisions. Doing so augments our personal agency, well-being, and resilience.

When practiced across communities, imaginatively working with the future builds what researchers call *social resilience.* Increasingly recognized as critical to navigating intense and unpredictable change, social resilience is a group's ability to cope with adversity, adapt to challenges, and build shared prosperity over time.[5] When imagining different futures becomes a collaborative process, the results augment our adaptive capacities.[6] Developing shared visions requires and builds trust, cultivating the kinds of connections that help societies weather the unpredictable.[7]

Negotiating modern change demands the personal and social resilience that imagination fosters. Technological, political, and climatic disruption will only accelerate in coming years. How these changes will play out over time defies prediction—there are too many inputs beyond our control.

And that's entirely the point. The future isn't ours to predict. It's ours to imagine and create, together.

This book argues that speculative futures provides essential, practical approaches to creating resilient cities. Its tools empower design professionals and urban residents alike to work with the future today, democratizing development as a result. I focus on cities not because more rural areas are unimportant, but because cities are home to the majority of the world's population. At present, 55 percent of all people live in cities.[8] By the 2050s, researchers estimate those numbers will grow to nearly 70 percent, adding another 2.5 billion people to urbanized areas. Creating more resilient cities means building more resilient futures.

I have four goals in writing this. The first is to spell out the current limits of speculation in city planning, introduce the field of speculative futures, and articulate how its imaginative focus and accessible qualities increase individual and societal resilience. The second is to identify how speculative futures balances short-term needs with long-term change, reorienting our understanding of cities toward more adaptive capacity. The third is to show that by supporting cooperation over persuasion, speculative futures creates more collaborative and equitable development. The fourth is to explore how speculative futures shifts our collective imagination toward resilient possibility and cultivates proactive planning as a result.

Using speculative futures alone won't solve the many problems our cities face. Its power depends on how its tools are harnessed and to what ends. But if we—both urban professionals and all those who live in cities—can start to accept that the futures we design for are constantly in flux, we can get closer to creating the more resilient spaces we need to embrace what's headed our way.

Speculative futures helps us to not just recognize those inherently shifting contexts but also to actively imagine and cocreate what can be. The more we speculate about coming decades, the clearer our future visions become. The clearer our visions become, the more effectively we can find consensus on how to meet the challenges of twenty-first-century life. The tools of speculative futures empower us to push beyond the confines we place on our imaginations and build the resilient cities we need.

1

THE CASE FOR IMAGINATION

THE FIRST TIME I saw speculative futures used to shape cities, I was standing on the work. It was an April evening years ago, and I was headed to a client meeting. I hustled from my car toward the building in question, my arms full of rolled paper, when I noticed a series of questions chalked in block letters on the sidewalk.

I wish this was _____ the words called out. A statement followed by an empty line, stretching like an invitation.

The sidewalk fronted an empty lot surrounded by a chain link fence. Save for a few clumps of grass and plastic bags, the lot was empty. The sidewalk in front of it, however, was full. Chalked statements spread across the cracked pavement, each starting with the same phrase: *I wish this was* _____. Pieces of chalk lay scattered along the sidewalk's edge, which previous passersby had used to fill in the blanks. *I wish this was* A PARK. *I wish this was* A GARDEN. *I wish this was* A GLOW IN THE DARK DANCE FLOOR.

I later learned that the effort was a replica of work by the artist Candy Chang. She had done a series of public installations in the mid-2000s, pasting stickers on vacant city buildings in New Orleans.[1] Each was printed with the words *I wish this was* _____. Her stickers were a question and statement both, transforming boarded-up windows and weathered siding into spaces where people shared their dreams about what could be. It was a simple kind of speculative futures approach, an invitation to ask, "What if?" and "Why not?"

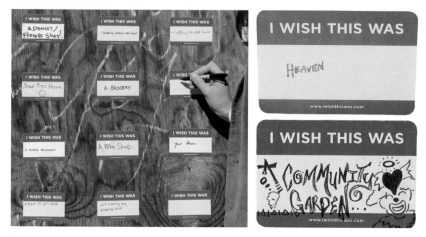

Community ideas collected through Candy Chang's "I Wish This Was" project in New Orleans, LA (2010).

Standing on the sidewalk that April evening, staring at the words chalked on the ground, I didn't understand that bigger context. I didn't know Chang existed. I didn't know that "what if?" questions were fundamental to the speculative futures field. I didn't know what speculative futures was. I just thought the phrases were a playful way to spark public conversation about the vacant lot's future. People were voluntarily—happily, it seemed—brainstorming what the site could be.

I wanted to join, to skip the scheduled client meeting and add my ideas to the growing list. Since I also didn't want to lose my job, I hurried toward the building instead.

———————

Asking what people want vacant lots to become is one of many reasons to use speculative futures. Silicon Valley companies apply the tools to prototype new technologies. International governments harness them to shape long-term development strategies. Hollywood studios ensure the success of franchises like *Star Wars* and the Marvel Cinematic Universe by building on their principles.

The various approaches form an amorphous field, with little agreement on definitions or applications. To steal the words of researchers Shelley Streeby, Nalo Hopkinson, and Christopher Fan, I've come to understand speculative futures as "an umbrella . . . under which a wide range of strategies for world-making and imagining the future . . . are situated."[2] Although the tactics under the umbrella are distinct, they all use story-based speculation to explore alternative worlds. Peering into the future is a skill that sparks reflection on current conditions and the long-term ramifications of where decisions can lead.

It's this gap between fantasy and reality that's both where imagination lives and where real change can occur.[3] Imagination massages the space between what could be and what is, transforming future uncertainties and hopes into present-day choices. Speculative futures harnesses imagination to translate fantasy into reality.

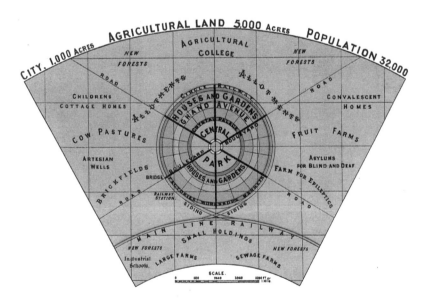

Diagram of Ebenezer Howard's Garden City (1902).

For people involved in the work of building cities, that gap is familiar. Urban planning is a speculative storytelling exercise, one where alternative versions of city space are explored, evaluated, and enacted over time. Designers and architects envision new possibilities for districts, transit systems, and plazas, then work to build them in physical form.

Historically, the space between fantasy and reality has been key to promoting idealized visions of city life. Ebenezer Howard's nineteenth-century plan of the Garden City was a speculative vision of what he saw as necessary change. This was 1898, at the tail end of the first wave of the Industrial Revolution, when urban centers were plagued by overcrowding, pollution, and disease. Howard proposed a radical alternative—move people out to the country and have them commute to work by railroad, trams, and (eventually) cars. While his Garden City started off as an imaginary suburban ideal, he presented it as such a convincing solution that it soon dominated city-making throughout the twentieth century.

Speculating about the future to predict and persuade is still a dominant part of how cities are made today. In 2020, the Danish architect Bjarke Ingels released a plan for the entire Earth. Titled Masterplanet, the project attempts to show that humanity can use already-existing technologies to have both a sustainable footprint on the planet and a high quality of life.[4] While this kind of visionary thinking is inspiring, it promotes the faulty

Aerial view of Boston in 1860 by J. W. Black (left) and Utah suburbia in 2019 by M. Tusznynski (right). Howard's Garden City was a blueprint for the shift toward suburbia that dominated much of the twentieth century.

belief that the right blend of technological tools, spatial strategies, and expertise inevitably leads to good solutions. A recent review of the project in *Time* magazine pointed out that "even in a world where the COVID-19 pandemic has transformed our understanding of what is possible in terms of collective responses to a global challenge, it's all but impossible to imagine any single climate plan achieving meaningful uptake from industries, governments and communities around the world."[5] Like Howard over a century ago, Ingels focuses on the power of technological tactics and land-use strategies to predict a potential future and persuade others to agree.

I spent years of my career using speculation in similar ways—focused on prediction and persuasion. After walking past the words chalked on the sidewalk that April evening, for example, I devoted the rest of the night to limiting the kinds of dialogue the chalk words had inspired. A coworker and I set up for the meeting by running around the conference room, hanging swaths of paper from its cinder-block walls. Our boss was already with the developer funding the project, shaking hands, drinking wine from a plastic cup, and describing how well the project was going. We rushed to finish before they appeared, our footsteps thudding across the concrete floor as we filled the walls with visuals to make our proposal appear as commanding as it could be.

An "Innovation Center" in a college town, the concept was relatively simple. It would repurpose a couple hundred acres outside the town center, redeveloping a swath of agricultural land into a site for research, prototyping, and light manufacturing. Residential space would let workers live on-site, with retail and office areas included in the mix. By integrating different uses so close together, the pitch went, the site would become a place where innovations made at the local college could be tested and brought to market, keeping recent graduates in town and growing the city in size, reputation, and tax base.[6]

The client had been excited by the initial idea and commissioned us for the more detailed plans we were set to present. Our team had spent months on city zoning codes, population demographics, and financial models in preparation. We massed out version after version of district layouts to make sure we were taking advantage of solar gains and winter winds. We plotted out plantings that would keep the area green and cool during hot summer months. We rendered everything in images with blue skies and smiling people.

When my boss began the pitch that evening, he started the conversation as he often did when selling a project—by pointing to those blue-sky images as if the futures they depicted were about to occur. Just raise the money and approve the plans, his gestures implied, and the smiling people would appear. Because we didn't want to seem as if we had an agenda, we included other options along with the main proposal. It was a typical tactic. Shared alternatives were always less developed, sometimes left in sketch form, and rarely populated with people, let alone people who smiled. We knew the decisions we thought were best and pushed clients toward them accordingly, our visuals the manifestation of our bias.

We had reason to push for as little interference as possible. Cultivating a compelling vision of what doesn't exist requires more than imagination. It demands funding and support. An idea without the backing to bring it to life is just another idea. And backing is easiest to secure when the proposal at hand doesn't offer a mere possibility of success, but a guarantee. Presenting a project as a certainty is a safer bet.

Yet certainty isn't safe. Projects billed as solid regularly fall short of their original promises. Schemes that initially appear sure-fire can't always adapt to climatic changes, pandemics, demographic shifts, or funding gaps. For all its presentation-based assurance, the Innovation Center eventually faltered as well. While the client approved the work that April night and funded the next round of plans, it wasn't long before he called my boss to say that economic factors had changed and the effort would have to go on hold. Even if the center had been built, it was primed to lead to conflict. The closest our team had come to engaging the city's communities was asking the planning department for preliminary feedback on permits. We weren't trying to cultivate dialogue about the changes we hoped to enact.

The chalk on the sidewalk next to that empty lot used imagination to provide what the Innovation Center lacked—space for public collaboration. The work didn't depend on planners presenting an idealized goal or facilitating a particular process. It wasn't a means to persuade people about what should occur. It was a forum for conversation. It used something that most everyone can understand—words on the ground—to invite those who called the city home to envision its future for themselves.

Speculative futures widens the spectrum of who gets to shape the future and to what ends. It does this by making the future personal. Facing large-scale, long-term change can be daunting. Problems like global contagion or economic inequality are so complex that it can be hard to believe any intervention might make a difference.

Working through fears of what could be depends on connecting with the abstract. Linking issues like climate change, for example, with the realities of our own neighborhoods, jobs, and relationships, translates conceptual ideas into concrete emotions. Thinking of how the beaches we love might disappear, how more frequent floods might destroy our homes, or how we might have to move to flee mounting wildfire risk, evokes feelings like anger, sadness, or guilt—feelings that inspire us to act. A recent study found that when people feel personally affected by potential climatic change, they are more likely to support carbon mitigation efforts and push for proactive policies.[7] Forming emotional connections to potential futures helps us move from denial and despair to action.

Proactively imagining the future in personal ways ultimately increases our resilience. When we engage with what could be, we grow psychologically stronger. Professor of psychology Martin Seligman laid out the case in a 2021 interview for the *New York Times,* describing how exploring the future cultivates both optimism and personal agency. When people imagine the future, he explained, their efforts are promoted "by a set of brain circuits that juxtapose time and space and get [them] imagining things well and beyond the here and now."[8] The higher resolution a person's understanding of the future, the more powerful their future visioning and learning skills become.

Using imagination to take the long view to heart makes us stronger, more resilient individuals. Seligman articulated the argument in a 2017 opinion piece, insisting that connecting to the future through the lens of curiosity increases our capacities to learn. According to Seligman, that learning happens "not by storing static records but by continually retouching memories and imagining future possibilities."[9] The farther into the future we look, the more frequently we challenge current conventions and assumptions. The more we challenge assumptions, the more our senses of autonomy and resilience expand.

When we imagine our futures with other people, we build critical stores of social resilience. The ability to navigate societal and ecological change of all kinds,[10] social resilience is what tells us who needs help and how to reach them when life turns upside down. Regular interaction, trust, and connection with the places and institutions where we live are what make it stronger. When our communities are more socially resilient, we're better able to self-organize, advocate for our demands, and cope with the increasingly unpredictable events of modern life.[11]

How we imagine and build cities—and who is involved in the process—dictates whether social resilience shrinks or expands. When urban planning is more collaborative, it demands more patience and empathy between participants, a process that, by necessity, cultivates greater degrees of trust.[12] Our abilities to collaborate stem largely from our capacities to imagine. As philosopher Martha Nussbaum puts it, our imaginations enable us to acknowledge "those who are other than ourselves, both in concrete circumstances and even in thought and emotion."[13] Imagination is what enables us to place ourselves in other people's shoes and see life from different perspectives. It's what gives us understanding and faith in other people, allowing trust, cooperation, and social resilience to grow.[14]

During emergencies, social resilience can be the difference between life and death. In a 2013 article, professor of sociology Eric Klinenberg illustrates the idea through the story of the 1995 Chicago heat wave. The event was intense, killing over seven hundred people across the city. In two adjacent neighborhoods, however, the impacts were strikingly different. Both were poor areas with many older residents, yet one, Englewood, had a death rate of thirty-three out of every hundred thousand people, while the other, Auburn Gresham, had a death rate of three out of every hundred thousand. Klinenberg found that social ties made the critical difference. The Auburn Gresham neighborhood was full of small businesses that drew older residents, a population particularly vulnerable to heat waves, out into the public realm. They had more regular interactions with fellow community members as a result, creating more robust social infrastructures. When the heat wave hit, Auburn Gresham residents knew who needed help and where to reach them. They had built the social connections they needed to face the extreme.

Social resilience is our first and most critical tool for negotiating disruption and change. While strong physical infrastructure—sewer systems, storm-surge barriers, and electrical grids—is undeniably essential, a community's strength is largely dictated by the strength of its social ties. And while updating transit networks and water mains depends on large funds and spans of time, cultivating connections with our neighbors and the institutions that support us can happen right now. Proactively engaging with the future helps us begin.

Speculative futures increases our resilience by inviting us to reflect on the trajectories of our own lives.[15] It doesn't interrogate the future to push a vision of what should be. It focuses on provocation instead, on acknowledging that how we see the world fundamentally shapes the futures we see. Rather than asking us to connect with the implications of coming change on our own, the tools of speculative futures create high-resolution versions of how daily life could evolve. The approaches ask how a noodle shop gets bulk food delivered in 2040. They explore what going to the bathroom might be like in 2058. They show what a store would be like in 2130 if money no longer existed. They investigate how the systems and contexts of a particular time frame affect where people sleep or how they find partners to date. What's different? What do the differences make us feel? What alternatives would we prefer?

The field explores potential answers through a range of tools. Identifying scenarios is a primary approach. Developed in the mid-twentieth century, scenarios are essentially short, research-based stories serving as snapshots of potential conditions. From military strategy to business development, many sectors rely on scenarios to mitigate risk from possible change. Speculative futures employs them to creatively envision alternative worlds.

One of the inventors of the scenario approach, Herman Kahn, used them to plan for nuclear Armageddon. This was during the height of the Cold War, when thinking about life after an attack was as emotionally difficult as it was necessary. Kahn—an employee at the RAND Corporation[16] and a science fiction fan from a young age—used stories to think about the unthinkable. He called these stories "scenarios." To Kahn, a good scenario didn't simply dive into any possible future. It had to focus "on a possibility that would be important if it occurred."[17] Once he deemed a scenario as both likely and important, accuracy became far less essential than communicating viable impact. It was all about writing a convincing story. His efforts led to some of the first national-policy uses of scenario thinking in the United States, now a fundamental part of all futures work.

Speculative design emerged toward the end of the twentieth century. Coined by industrial design professors Anthony Dunne and Fiona Raby, the approach uses design to "challenge narrow assumptions, preconceptions and givens about the role products play in everyday life."[18] By interacting with objects and services created for "what if?" scenarios, people engage with different visions of the future, gaining tangible experiences of different

The em-muzzle from Anthony Dunne and Fiona Raby's "Spymaker" project (2006-2007).

approaches to being in the world.[19] Those experiences provide tactile information for reconsidering attitudes baked into the status quo. Dunne and Raby's 2006 Spymaker project, for example, designed a tool—what they called an "em-muzzle"—that used existing mass surveillance technology to train dogs to guide their owners to electronically unmonitored zones. Never intended for public use, the point of the em-muzzle was to get people thinking about how mass surveillance already infiltrates daily life, and provoke ethical, social, and political dialogue about possible alternatives.

Design fictions appeared in the mid-2000s. In the words of one of their originators,[20] designer Julian Bleecker, design fictions are "part story, part material, part idea-articulating prop, part functional software."[21] They're a more physical way to tell stories about the future. Creating a prototype of a tool that might occur in a given scenario cultivates tactile conversation about how that future might impact people's lives.[22]

Bleecker illustrated the concept with a project titled "Slow Messenger." The idea was to create a tool where "instant" messages would transmit over long stretches of time. The more someone carried the Slow Messenger device with them, the more of the message they would ultimately see. A Slow Messenger tool left by itself would be a sign that the owner didn't have much need or connection with the message, which would make the words take longer to appear. Bleecker designed the project to explore different rituals that could make digital communication feel more intimate. "If we make communication much slower," he asked in a blog post, "what do we learn about new ways of relating and sharing with our friends and loved ones?"[23] Does communication have to happen quickly to be impactful?

Of the many projects that have used design fictions over the years, one of my favorites is Hyphen-Labs' NeuroSpeculative AfroFeminism (NSAF) Salon. The three-part digital narrative re-envisions a Black hair salon as a lab for neurocosmetology, in which Black women use hair care to pioneer techniques for cognitive enhancement. Salon products, developed as design fictions, range from "sunblock for traveling through the multiverse, to earrings embedded with cameras that offer protection and visibility."[24] It's an afrofuturistic vision that increases its impact through the nuanced design of its details.[25]

Futurists Stuart Candy and Jake Dunagan began to champion experiential futures in the late 2000s. A way of translating the future into three-dimensional space, experiential futures are immersive scenarios, employing role-play and simulation to provide multisensory understanding of the potential future at hand. In Candy's words, "An experiential scenario is a future brought to life."[26] The two developed the approach when working on a project called Hawaii 2050.[27] Hoping to foster more public engagement in the state's long-term sustainability plan, the collaborators created four versions of how Hawaii might operate by the middle of the century and rented out a convention center for a community kick-off event. Participants, including policymakers and constituents, moved through four rooms, each containing an immersive experience of one of the four scenarios. Scenes ranged from a naturalization ceremony for climate change refugees to an information session at a well-being facility for technologically enhanced humans. Reflection sessions, held after participants engaged with the experiences, helped people debate and discuss long-term trajectories for the islands and their greater sustainability aims.

Lisa Jackson's Biidaaban: First Light VR still, National Film Board of Canada (2018).

Some experiential futures exist strictly in the digital world. "Biidaaban: First Light," for example, used virtual reality to explore an intensely different future for the city of Toronto. Created in 2018 by First Nation artist Lisa Jackson, the interactive virtual space enveloped viewers in a world transformed by climate change. Biidaaban's Toronto is a wetter city, where floods are more frequent and temperatures are warmer. Animals make nests in warehouses and alleys, while people grow food on skyscraper rooftops and commute by canoe. Text written in the languages of different First Nation peoples, including the Wendat, Kanien'kehá:ka (Mohawk) and Anishinaabe (Ojibway), appear in various areas of the city. When participants train their eyes on the text, they hear those languages spoken out loud, connecting to Toronto's early inhabitants in the process. The project provokes discussion about how dynamics toward nature in cities are shifting, encouraging people to ask whether different directions might be preferable instead.

In 2011, former Intel futurist Brian David Johnson popularized science fiction prototyping (SFP). Rather than designing objects, spaces, and experiences as types of critique, SFP relies more strictly on narrative to explore the implications of possible futures. Fictions are told through a range of mediums, from comic books and written stories to reports and short films, envisioning tools and environments as they'd be used in people's day-to-day lives. While SFP is most widely employed to test the impacts of emerging technologies, exploring how new inventions can shape and be shaped by those who use them, the approach is gaining traction outside of tech as well, across sectors from science communication to business development.

One of the SFP examples Johnson regularly highlights is *Star Trek*. A lot of today's commonplace tools—like tablet computers or devices that translate language in real time—were first depicted on the show in the 1960s. *Star Trek* also portrayed a slightly more racially progressive and gender-equal future compared to conditions when it first aired, articulating an alternative trajectory of how society could evolve. It was a fiction that let people dream, pointing out absurdities in the way things were done at the time and questioning aspects of culture then taken as a given.

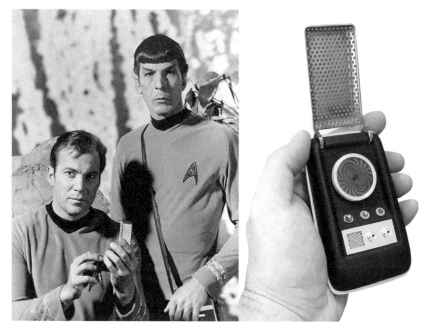

Star Trek characters Captain Kirk and Spock using a "communicator" (left) designed by Wah Chang (right), which served to influence forthcoming generations of cellphones.

The various speculative futures tools listed above all stem in some way from the more ancient practice of worldbuilding. Widely associated with films, books, television, and games, worldbuilding is a means of exploring the geographic, social, cultural, political, and ecological factors of alternate realities. J. R. R. Tolkien grounded his *Lord of the Rings* saga with detailed histories of the hobbits, humans, elves, dwarves, and orcs living within. Each had specific cultures, languages, and social customs, which Tolkien dutifully recorded in encyclopedic appendices. Yet worldbuilding is also the basis for mythology throughout human history, from the Greek gods of Mount Olympus to the contours of Aztec religion. It's a process where imaginary realities adhere to organized systems, where deities have logic and driving needs, where seasons move in accordance to overarching rules.

Where other speculative futures approaches often focus on distinct sequences of time, worldbuilding[28] constructs coherent, detailed, and consistent worlds. The more detailed a world becomes, the more questions it can be asked, providing increasingly nuanced understanding of potential repercussions and opportunities enacted by potential change. Because it articulates spaces with strong rules, histories, climatic contexts, and social dynamics, worldbuilding provides a framework for multiple participants to share and link their stories. As such, worldbuilding can serve as a powerful means of collaboration across disciplines, backgrounds, and beliefs.

Each type of speculative futures has its particular value. As design fictions largely focus on creating props and objects to articulate what future conditions could be, they work well for in-person or web-based projects. Speculative design is more comprehensive, allowing additional space for humor or the bizarre to invite people deeper into future-planning work. SFP brainstorms new tools, systems, and tech by merging fiction with iteration, making it particularly beloved in business circles. Because experiential futures places people in future scenes to augment their sensory and emotional responses, it can have particular potency when encountered face-to-face. Scenario generation, a foundation of all futures research, provides short windows into future conditions. With its focus on creating coordinated levels of detail, some worldbuilding is necessary in all efforts to give deeper form and shape to the futures at hand.

Approaches can be powerful when mixed and matched together. A few already form the basis of speculation in conventional urban design. The failed Innovation Center project I worked on combined two types: scenarios and speculative design.

Scenario development came first. The developer who hired us had a five- to ten-year time frame in mind, so that's the time frame we adopted. Within five years, 212 acres would transform from farmland into research, development, prototyping, and manufacturing facilities. Technology institutions would cluster together amid green lawns and shady trees, connecting start-ups, business incubators, and accelerators stemming from research at the local college. Ideally, scenarios are pathways to move beyond innate cognitive biases, acknowledge impending uncertainties, and make more informed decisions about where to go. They often stay in the "snapshot" space, describing conditions in a given future time frame without getting into why or how they evolved.[29] We took a narrower approach with the Innovation Center project, crafting a narrative window into a future designed to be as irresistible as possible.

Speculative design helped us dive into the scenario's details. It allowed us to ask what farmland on the edge of town would be like if transformed into a research and development center. Would people live there as well as work? How would transportation access operate? Grounding the project scenario with speculative design helped encourage our client—and the small numbers of community members with whom we engaged—to debate what parts of that future they did or didn't want. What types of buildings would best support a thriving innovation space? What was the right mix of office, research, and prototyping space? Should rooms all be designed to be flexible, so uses and programming could change as needed over time? Answering those questions and designing the fictional, proposed spaces that resulted made our speculative future feel increasingly real. The more real it felt, the easier it was to sell.

Incorporating a wider array of speculative futures tools can push urban development toward more provocative and accessible explorations of how the future can evolve. The words I found chalked on the sidewalk before the client meeting, for example, combined speculative design with experiential futures. By simply leaving space for others to finish the sentence *I wish this was _____*, the project became a public reimagining of what the empty lot could be.

Asking people to write down their ideas was a low-tech form of speculative design. Scrawling out visions on the street was a way of inviting people to inhabit potential futures in real time. Write out an alternative future in front of the space where it could occur and you got to step into that potential reality not just in your mind, but with your body.

Chalking the words on the street made the future experiential by making it interactive. The blank lines invited arrays of people to participate, to share their own visions and explore those left by others. It was a way of sparking civic collaboration through collective imagination. It didn't ultimately lead to any long-term, tangible impact—today the lot is a new housing development—but that doesn't mean the tactic had no value. Its use of narrative and experiential approaches inspired dozens of people to share visions of futures they wanted to see. It was a reminder that imagining the future is something everyone has the skills and insight to do. We just need space to begin.

––––––––––

Speculative futures makes cities more resilient by making urban development more accessible, inviting, and fun. Unlike more predictive or persuasion-focused ways of working with what's ahead, the tools help people actively engage the future through imagination and play. Future visions made by people untrained in disciplines like architecture might not always be particularly nuanced, but such critiques miss the point. Making the future approachable widens the breadth of how cities are planned, who they're planned for, and what kind of futures they embrace. While the tools can employ sophisticated technology, like virtual reality, they can also be simple. Chalking words on the ground can be just as effective as creating a digital experience. The point is to ask, "What else can exist in place of what is here right now?" The only essential ingredient to answering that question is imagination.

To borrow a phrase from Stuart Candy, when we don't just look ahead but also feel ahead, we illuminate and critique the kinds of baked-in beliefs that limit our imagination of how time can unfold. Internalizing the potential impacts of future change helps determine the trajectories that we actually want to take, spurring the future-thinking mentalities that increase resilience at individual levels and inspire more collaboration at civic scales. The more we understand the social, technological, environmental, and scientific changes that are radically transforming urban spaces, the more agency we have in shaping where we want to go. The more we share those ideas with each other, the stronger our collective visions become.[30]

Becoming fluent in the approaches of speculative futures empowers more of us to articulate, believe in, and enact our own futures. By emphasizing narrative connection, speculative futures embraces the fact that storytelling is more than just a way to entertain. It's a means of investigating our values, hopes, dreams, and fears about the ramifications of coming change.[31] Embracing speculative futures supports design that makes our humanity—our hunger for love, connection, and meaning—the foundation of how to test what coming years might hold. Valuing imagination, fantasy, and play as serious tools imbues possibility and resilience into the conversation of what is yet to be.

POSSIBILITY THROUGH PLAY

"... HEAR ... CLOSE ... SCHOOLS!"

I could hear the shouts long before I reached the meeting. It was almost seven in the evening, an hour past the official start time. I was late. Signs on the walls read "School District Meeting in the Gym," but they weren't necessary. Voices rang through the building, leading the way on their own. I slipped through one of the gym's side doors just as a middle-aged Black woman began to speak in the center of the room.

"If you're going to *change* these schools," she said, lingering over the word *change,* "you need to tell us exactly what you plan to do with them."

The woman sat straight-backed on one of the many folding chairs spread across the floor. Like the people around her, she held a plate of hot food in her lap, filled from containers arranged on a table at the main entrance. Attendees ate as they listened, their eyes darting toward the row of school district employees seated at the far end of the gym. Most of the people in the audience were Black or Brown. Many of the district employees, like me, were white.

I pulled my notebook and pen from my bag. I was there to observe. The firm I worked for was helping the district, a sprawling area across the bay from San Francisco, make a new plan for its facilities. The last plan, completed six years before, was never enacted. Former executives had used bond money meant to fund the projects on downtown office rentals and administrative services instead, leaving residents enraged, work undone, and the district mired in scandal. Schools had paint peeling from their walls, plumbing in need of repair, and aging cooling systems unequipped for increasingly frequent heat waves. Some of the untended buildings had already been closed for years, shut down when local students started transitioning to the area's growing array of charter schools.

Those already closed spaces were the focus of the night's meeting. What to do with them? Let them stay as they were? Vote on a new bond for repairs? Lease them out for another agency to renovate and raise funds for the school district in the process?

Residents' concerns ran high. "How do we know you would actually lease these buildings?" one older man wanted to know. "How do we know you're not going to sell them to some developer?"

"If you're going to redevelop these spaces, they need to be affordable housing," a woman in a loose-knit cap insisted. "How can we trust you're going to help us with that?"

If you've gone to a community meeting, this kind of scene might feel familiar. Whether initiated by a school district, a planning department, or a utility provider, public forums often raise fears that what's proposed will enact more harm than help. Government bureaucracies can be time consuming and frustrating to engage. Members of the public often assume they'll have to push back hard to make sure their priorities are heard. It's easy to feel like the planning process is more of a battle than a chance for positive change.

Speculative futures works with these fraught dynamics by harnessing the power of play. Focusing on the possibilities the future might bring creates space to temporarily set present tensions aside. Existing issues aren't ignored. Rather, they're contextualized within the fact that they won't necessarily last forever. Even if the present feels impossible to change, the future is still unwritten. Taking the time to envision and refine alternative futures can foster a potent kind of openness. Imaginative play is fertile ground for collaborative visioning to unfold.

A neighborhood in western Amsterdam took this lesson to heart in 2014, transforming their public square into a micro-nation. Over the course of three months, Columbusplein—the name of the square in question—became the officially sanctioned Republic of Columbusplein, a nation-state complete with its own flag, passport, and stamps.

The micro-nation was an attempt to address social issues that had plagued the neighborhood for years. With residents from countries as diverse as Morocco, Dominica, and Surinam, neighborhood dynamics were often charged. From bullying to cultural differences to gang violence, tension shaped the area's character.[1] Fourteen public agencies had tried to address the neighborhood's problems over the years, implementing both support programs and stricter punishment systems—all with limited success.[2]

The micro-nation concept emerged as an alternative approach. Rather than physically redesigning the neighborhood, the effort sought to shift people's attitudes about what was possible. An artist named Jorge Mañes Rubio facilitated the effort with a group of local residents and social workers, developing interactive programs to translate the concept into lived experience. They created a national space program. They led residents in

Graphic lines on the ground of the local basketball court (left) informed the graphic that became the Republic of Columbusplein flag (right), J. M. Rubio (2014).

competitions to develop an official flavor of dipping sauce. They made the experience of living in the micro-nation imaginative and playful both.

Play is fun, but it's also an important way to explore. Play is a space to investigate and express feelings, to test out different ideas and ways of solving problems. When play takes on clear constraints—rules by which players must abide—it takes on more nuance, richness, and form.[3] Kids build entire worlds with detailed rules to play their games, using the simplest of tools. Sticks can be magic wands or swords or light sabers. Pieces of cloth can be invisibility cloaks or an eagle's wings. Cardboard boxes can transform into towering castles or deep mountain caverns, places to go on death-defying adventures without leaving home. The more detailed a play world is, the more it allows its players to explore the ramifications of seeing in entirely different ways. Play mixed with constraint is worldbuilding.

By nurturing innate predilections for play, the tools of speculative futures help people temporarily look beyond the confines of existing conditions. When we stay mired in the problems that define so many of today's issues, it can be difficult—even impossible—to believe in the potential for

Design fictions created for the Republic of Columbusplein included passport (left), money (middle), and stamps (right), J. M. Rubio (2014).

positive change. Injecting the planning process with play can release seemingly entrenched degrees of tense and long-standing struggle. In Columbusplein, translating an imaginary world into three-dimensional life gave a conflict-ridden community new belief. Reframing the neighborhood as a nation with its own customs and identity reoriented residents' relationships both to the square and to each other. Play generated connection and cooperation between factions previously at odds.

The sense of possibility fostered in the Republic of Columbusplein was not present at the school district meeting. Community members were anxious. Their neighborhood was already changing. Rising rents threatened their ability to stay in their homes. And now the district wanted to permanently transform schools that had only recently closed? How could they believe that the school property—public property—would be leased out in ways that would help rather than make things worse?

District employees had their own agenda to promote. The new superintendent, hired in the wake of the scandal, had ideas beyond simply executing the previous facilities plan. The number of charter schools in the district was exploding at the time, pulling students and resources away from the public system. Many of the remaining programs were crammed into overcrowded spaces, while others had far fewer kids than their buildings were designed to hold. What they needed to do, the new superintendent insisted, was consolidate the less-populated programs into facilities closest to where students lived. That would shorten commutes and build stronger connections around the schools. The newly vacant sites could be leased for housing or commercial use, which would provide the school district with much-needed income.

That's where my firm came in. We were helping the facilities team figure out which school buildings could best be used in other ways. Which were located closest to transit lines that could work well as subsidized housing for teachers? Which could serve as local business incubators? Who was the kind of real estate developer who could raise private funds to push things forward? We spent months developing ideas of how the process could unfold, how sites might be identified, who potential partners might be.

Deciding how to involve members of the community was a critical yet delicate ingredient. Alienating residents, everyone agreed, would be disastrous. If people felt threatened or left out, they could waylay efforts indefinitely. Only when we had stress tested the reallocation process across a slew of school district departments did we initiate conversations with community members. School officials wanted to take the temperature of what residents thought to see how they might react.

Starting with the buildings that had already been closed for years seemed like the best way to begin. What would residents think about reusing those facilities for non-school purposes? Could they see those moves as potentially beneficial? We could shift our messaging depending on the response. We wouldn't necessarily change the plan, but we could change the way we talked about it.

Community members weren't impressed with the pitch. "You've said plenty of things in the past that haven't been true," a young woman stated later that night. "How can we trust what you say now is what's actually going to happen?"

The audience erupted into a long applause. Amid the din, a school official insisted that those transgressions were in the past, that transparency and accountability were the focus moving forward.

"We don't believe you!" a man yelled back.

Residents at the meeting had good reason to be wary. Like many urban areas today, the school district's city was gentrifying fast. A center of Black culture in the San Francisco Bay Area for over half a century, the city had been home to people like Angela Davis and Alice Walker. Today, with housing costs rising and new development planned, the affordability that once enabled people of color to prosper in the area is rapidly disappearing. Home prices are now quadruple of what they were just two decades ago. Renovated homes typically sell above $1 million, affordable only for the wealthy or well-connected.[4] As generational wealth and class are deeply racial issues in the United States, well-off and well-connected people are much more likely to be white than Black or Brown.

The city's current rates of gentrification have direct ties to exclusive planning practices of the past. Inequalities initiated by old, top-down urban planning projects have created conditions in which many current developments—often intended to improve conditions with new housing or parks or commercial centers—cause property values and lifestyle costs to increase, marginalizing and displacing long-term residents in the process.[5] Discrimination enacted decades ago makes new construction likely to exacerbate rates of gentrification, forcing people to move, fracturing social and economic safety nets, and creating new degrees of vulnerability in communities already at risk.[6]

The issues have roots stretching back more than a century, back to Ebenezer Howard's Garden City. When Howard published his vision of uniform, bucolic city life in 1898, urban practitioners quickly adopted the premise and proselytized its value.[7] Howard's symmetrical plans translated into regimented designs of vertical housing and green parks, with rigid divisions between residential, commercial, and industrial space. Planning cities according to efficiency, function, and formula became the gold standard. Expanding standardized design, the argument went, would reinvent urban spaces as orderly, clean, well-oiled machines.[8] The modernist movement was born, remaking cities around the world.[9]

One of the cities that modernism indelibly transformed was San Francisco. Its redevelopment focused on one neighborhood in particular—the Fillmore. Today, the Fillmore is a predominantly white area,[10] yet it's a kind of lore in the Bay Area that if you could go back to the neighborhood in the early 1960s, you'd be in a nexus of Black life. You'd hear live music in the middle of open-air plazas. You'd see streets lined with Black-owned businesses—jewelers, florists, shoe shiners, and fish fries. You'd see people smoking on corners and strolling with shopping bags full of groceries. You'd see flyers for meetings of civil rights groups.[11] So many businesses, nightclubs, and restaurants flourished across the district that you would have called it what everyone else did—the Harlem of the West.[12]

City planning department documents described the
Fillmore as a neighborhood devasted by blight that
needed to be "reclaimed," SFCPC (1947).

To San Francisco's planners and wealthy white residents,[13] the Fillmore
was an eyesore. Officials were adamant that "cleaning up" the neighborhood's dense housing and street life was essential to making the city both
more beautiful and profitable. A planner hired to do an initial study in 1947
declared that "nothing short of a clean sweep and a new start can make
the district a genuinely good place in which to live."[14] Illustrated pamphlets
accompanying his final report painted a rosy picture of the neighborhood's
proposed makeover. Tree-lined walks and wide benches wrapped around
tidy apartment buildings. Recreation areas full of tennis and badminton
courts sat next to gently flowing fountains.[15] It was a narrow vision of what
ideal city life should be, a modernist vision. That the redesign was developed by a few white practitioners, isolated from the needs of the actual
Black community targeted for redevelopment, was not widely discussed.[16]

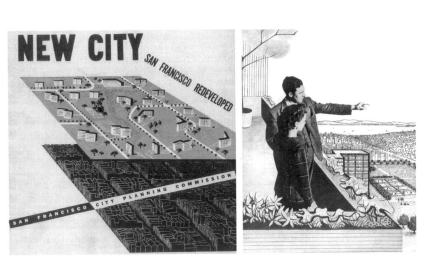

The San Francisco City Planning Commission's "New City" proposal for the Fillmore district (left) included designs depicting white residents enjoying "all the beauty and restfulness of the suburbs combined with all the advantages of the the City" (right), SFCPC (1947).

Despite public outcry, redevelopment sped ahead.[17] The main artery of the neighborhood was expanded from a two-lane street into a major boulevard. A new shopping complex replaced multi-family homes and dozens of Black-owned businesses.[18] By the end of the eighties, planners had transformed 108 acres, razing apartments, plazas, and side streets, and displacing over twenty thousand people. Many were resettled in substandard housing in polluted areas, initiating a migration of Black people from the city that San Francisco has yet to reverse. As a recent San Francisco Chronicle article described the situation today, "The Fillmore district has been gentrified to the point that an African American presence is almost nonexistent."[19] In the 1970s, Black people made up roughly 10 percent of San Francisco's population. Those numbers have since been cut in half. The Fillmore's Black community is now a ghost.

Many at the school board meeting were aware of this traumatic history. They lived in its shadow. Some knew people who had been displaced by what happened in the Fillmore. A few of the older residents might have been displaced themselves. They knew that whether by sudden demolition or the more incremental sweep of gentrification, displacement is stressful, disempowering, and has devastating effects on community health. Neighbors and friends are more likely to help each other find jobs, mentors, and places to live. These kinds of connections, studies show, grow over time to create greater degrees of trust, collective action, and civic participation.[20] Social ties create social resilience. When they facture, social resilience fractures as well.

Social psychiatrist Mindy Fullilove has described the harm enacted by urban renewal efforts of the past as "root shock." Because "people were stripped of their roots, and forced, without aid, to struggle through the period of shock to replant themselves as best they might,"[21] the disastrous impacts of redevelopment in places like the Fillmore resound just as loudly today.[22] Displacing and disenfranchising neighborhoods of color in inner-city areas disrupted generations of social capital and support. Modern rates of gentrification stem as much from inequities in who new projects are designed to benefit as from those earlier injustices.[23] It's why Black and Brown communities are less likely to own their own homes or have the funds to stay in areas with rising costs of living. It's why social resilience in countries like the United States is as much a racial issue as it is economic, political, and cultural.

The school district meeting wasn't designed to acknowledge those issues. District officials were focused on accelerating their own ideas for change instead. Eager to see if they could shift participants' mounting anger, they divided people into groups to fill out surveys and brainstorm potential redevelopment ideas. What kinds of resources did attendees want to see in their communities? If the buildings had to be repurposed, what would they want created?

I pulled a chair alongside one group to listen. One man wanted a commercial-grade kitchen where people could test recipes, potentially transforming sauces or preserves made at home into small businesses. A woman advocated for building housing for local teachers and other people in the community. A third person wanted closed schools to reopen, to be available to her grandchildren as they had been for her own kids when they were young.

When the brainstorming was over, people shared results. Some nodded their agreement when they heard something they liked. Others shouted approval. Vocal opposition was the most common response. "That will never work!" a gray-haired woman called out when a man shared his group's idea for a local health clinic. "They want to make money with these spaces!"

A blanket of frustration enveloped the room. Sidestepping long-standing conflict in favor of promoting new agendas makes cultivating trust and possibility difficult, if not impossible, to do.

Using speculative futures to inject planning with play offers a more collaborative path for city-making. Transforming complex tensions into ground for cocreation is possible. The Republic of Columbusplein project is proof. The fictional backbone of the effort created a context where people from different backgrounds were able to find common interest. In such a multicultural area, where many confessed to feeling torn between several identities, the speculative narrative of the micro-nation provided a focal point for a new kind of belonging.[24] The concept provided room for more trusting connections to grow, which in turn helped residents augment the positive potential that had been latent in their neighborhood all along.

Turning a public square into a micro-nation was far from a random idea. The city of Amsterdam had been trying to solve Columbusplein's social issues through more experimental efforts for years, beginning in 2011. The square, which had long been a hangout for local teenagers, was reshaped by government-supported cultural programs like "Mommy and Daddy in the Playground" days. Officials understood that shifting the space's identity could occur through social organizing. Getting children and parents to use the square started to alter people's ideas of how they could interact with neighborhood space.[25] Local organizations followed up with a "Fresh in Class" initiative, where team members moved through the neighborhood in the evenings, encouraging kids to get to bed so they wouldn't fall asleep in school or cause disruptions on the streets at night.

Space flights with tyvek kites (left) by members of the Columbusplein Space
Program (right), J. M. Rubio (2014).

By the time the Republic of Columbusplein came along in 2014, the
neighborhood's transformation was underway. The success of the previous programming initiatives encouraged the local government to continue support for more experimental projects. Officials agreed to a new
iteration, pairing artists and designers with existing institutions to come
up with short-term projects. Jorge Mañes Rubio, an Amsterdam-based
artist originally from Spain, was assigned to work in the West Amsterdam
area for a few months. Local politicians introduced him to the square and
its long-standing tensions and connected him with social workers operating on the ground.

The micro-nation concept was Rubio's creative extension of efforts already
happening on-site.[26] He wanted to understand what a different approach to
addressing neighborhood tensions might be, what he—an artist who would
only be in the area for a short time—could offer. Walking across the square's
basketball court one day, he noticed a suite of colored lines intersecting on
the ground. The pattern reminded him of the strong graphics typically used
on national flags, which made him think of nation-states. What if, he began
to wonder, the neighborhood became its own nation?

While Rubio came up with the nation-state concept on his own, he used
worldbuilding to invite locals to bring it to life. If the neighborhood was no
longer just part of West Amsterdam, but a country in its own right, what did

that mean? What kind of practices did they want to use to populate it? How would days in the Republic of Columbusplein differ from days in the square?

Design fiction and experiential futures helped them articulate the details. Their first effort was programming a competition for a national secret sauce for fries, a local favorite snack. The next was a space program. Young neighborhood astronauts got to visit the European Space Agency in nearby Noordwijk, learning about astronaut life in preparation for their own space flights back in Columbusplein using tyvek kites. They held the first Columbusplein Olympics, setting up mats for long-jump contests, ropes for tug-of-war battles, and serious games of soccer. Local police came out to cheer on the participants, showing support for residents who often saw them primarily as sources of oppression. As the months passed, the public square became a sanctioned micro-nation in its own right, acknowledged in Amsterdam and by other micro-nations worldwide.[27] Residents could imagine that they were citizens of their own shared nation-state and live out the ramifications of doing so in real time.

Local resident playing with a revised version of the Republic of Columbusplein flag during the micro-nation's Olympic Games, J. M. Rubio (2014).

The Republic of Columbusplein used play to emphasize the power of possibility over problem solving. Compared to most planning and design projects, it's a dramatically different tactic. By nature, urban design is a problem-focused discipline. When a street doesn't effectively accommodate traffic, it's slated for redesign. When a city lacks affordable housing, people have to figure out how to increase housing stock. When faced with Columbusplein's ongoing social tensions, many previous organizations had focused on addressing the problems. They developed punitive programs to ameliorate gang violence. They held community workshops where people could voice concerns. Until the micro-nation popped up, however, few of those efforts had invited residents to experience what living in a more collaborative neighborhood could be like. By fostering play, the micro-nation helped people look beyond existing problems and embody the potential of what could be.

Because speculative futures approaches like worldbuilding apply people's natural storytelling and play-based skills, they can be potent ways to increase collaboration on common goals. Asking "Why not?" is a means of challenging the status quo, of making space for people to explore alternatives, articulate preferences, and feel more empowered as a result.[28] Studies have found that the process of collaboratively or individually rewriting the narratives of existing realities can form the basis for powerful partnerships.[29] Young kids regularly make their own play worlds that still invite input and influence from others. It's a kind of cocreation that people intrinsically know how to do.

Play helps us reconcile differences in belief and attitude.[30] Because games inherently invite curiosity, exploration, and iteration, employing elements of play in urban planning cultivates powerful shifts in how people invest in the process. They let us explore the complexity of the problems our cities and communities face through a more imaginative lens. Fostering trust through the shared experiences that play provides engages people over the longer periods of time that enacting real change often requires.[31]

This is not to say that creating the micro-nation made all Columbusplein's issues disappear. It didn't. While crime rates have decreased, recent studies have found that social tensions are still present.[32] And while local leaders recognized the enthusiasm that the micro-nation concept sparked and supported the work accordingly,[33] the effort dissolved shortly after Rubio's tenure ended. He came to Columbusplein as an outside artist, interested more in trying new tactics to address social tensions than on understanding how or if those tactics should endure.

Reflecting on the effort in an interview years later, Rubio mused that finding ways to make the project more permanent could have helped. He had only a few months to devise and implement the micro-nation concept, and only so much funding to enact it. Things had to move quickly, leaving little time for building the trust it might have taken to cultivate more community buy-in from the start. Without that buy-in, it was clear to Rubio that once he stopped coming to the neighborhood, the micro-nation programs would stop as well. The social workers had their own programs to pursue. They didn't have the time, funding, or energy to keep the micro-nation going. Today the Republic of Columbusplein no longer exists beyond a few websites and the memories of those who helped to bring it to life.[34]

Despite its short duration, the micro-nation accomplished the radical feat of expanding what it meant to live around the square. It created a shared language, however temporary, for investment and cooperation to take root. The speculative futures tools used in the work harnessed residents' natural creativity and storytelling abilities in the service of a more empowered kind of collaboration. Instead of subsuming the cultural values and norms of different groups, the micro-nation became a space where people from diverse backgrounds, who already lived side by side, could develop a sense of shared identity that still made room for their differences. The micro-nation became a space where those who called the neighborhood home had the opportunity to shape what living within it meant.

Using play to work with conflict and inequality isn't easy. Creating spaces for people to envision and enact new realities takes effort. It takes commitment. Residents need to feel that doing so is both safe and worth their time. They need to believe their ideas will be taken seriously. The Republic of

Columbusplein was the product of months of work by people who believed in the power of not just a more collaborative future but also a more collaborative present.

The school district meeting lacked that kind of intention. District employees didn't have the time or money for such involved, sustained outreach. Play wasn't part of their job descriptions. They were there to get residents' agreement, not to spark imagination about potential futures.

Speculative futures tools wouldn't have guaranteed a better outcome for the meeting. They wouldn't have solved the issues created by generations of systemic racism. But they could have laid some groundwork for a different kind of future. They could have helped people find opportunities within existing difficulties. What if district officials had set up a less confrontational context, where residents didn't feel forced to defend their interests? What if attendees hadn't been asked to focus immediately on specific buildings, but were invited first to explore broader questions about changes they wanted to see? What if both sides prioritized identifying shared possibility over promoting their already-formed agendas? What if they created their own micro-nation to do so? What if and why not?

FINDING
OUR SENSES

IN 2017, THE GOVERNMENT of the United Arab Emirates (UAE) got a whiff of what its air might smell like in thirty years. Looking to develop long-term energy policy with a more creative approach, UAE ministers hired a speculative futures studio to provide a multisensory exploration of what life in 2050 could become. The studio in question, a firm named Superflux, designed an array of experiential futures they dubbed the Future Energy Lab.

Their "pollution machine" sat alongside an interactive energy simulator and a suite of role-playing games. Rather than reading about the noxious fumes that will develop if today's rates of fossil fuel use continue, participants could inhale them.[1] The combination of carbon monoxide, sulfur dioxide, and nitrogen dioxide made for a foul mix, a blend of acrid sweetness and rotten eggs.

Sniffing that putrid potential reality created a different way for UAE ministers to reflect on their country's future. They had seen plenty of data detailing how their oil-based economy creates environmental and public health issues. They knew the facts. The pollution machine provided a new,

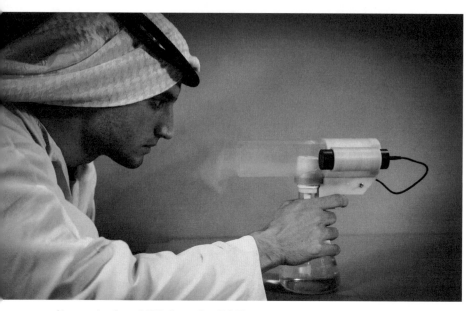

Air samples from 2050, Superflux (2017).

olfactory link to information they'd heard many times before. Soon after the Future Energy Lab ended, the UAE announced $163 billion in renewable energy investment.[2]

What exact part Superflux's work played in the UAE's decision-making process is unclear. Yet many of the people responsible for those decisions participated in the experiential futures installation. Breathing the noxious air that their children and grandchildren might breathe made that future tangible and present. It made the connection between today's decisions and tomorrow's reality visceral, personal, and close.

Feeling into the future is rare in urban development. Many projects adopt the opposite stance, creating plans based on the logic of present-day conditions. It's a tendency steeped in paradox. Proposed plans are alternative visions of what can be, literal manifestations of the fact that the future is always changing. Yet many projects approved for construction are designed for current contexts. Power grids, water mains, and buildings—infrastructure that lasts for decades—are rarely crafted to embrace shifts that happen over time. Mitigating existing risks is a far more frequent goal, enacting futures designed as extensions of today.

An early project of mine epitomized this kind of present-day focus. A brand-new city in China, it was a nineteen-square-mile expanse bordering an existing town. Although my team and I were tasked with designing the city from scratch, the site was far from empty. Pictures revealed small villages, narrow alleys, lurching cypress trees, and garden plots, spaces that our work would eventually erase. My firm planned new roads, waterways, tree canopies, and sewer lines at a rapid pace, conjuring a new town from conception through construction.

The client envisioned the area as a high-tech industrial zone, complete with glass-walled hotels, pleasure villas, and parks to draw tourists from afar. An existing lake, edged with low grasses and not a small amount of trash, would be remade into what local tourism websites were already calling the biggest park in the region. When complete, the ads promised, it would be "an ideal place to relax."[3] Our design team would fill it with artificial waterfalls, glass-bottomed walkways, and flower-edged boulevards, crafting the site into a recreational wonderland.

Building this new city required relocating long-term residents. It was a necessary part of the transition, my bosses explained, but it would only be temporary. When the housing was done, displaced families would be able to get new apartments, as would workers from neighboring areas. Everyone would have safe commutes to their jobs, greener homes, and cleaner air. Our town would start as a kind of bedroom community, with inhabitants taking high-speed trains to and from work. With time, the project lead insisted, the area would develop into a thriving hub of its own, a new kind of Chinese urban utopia. Until then, we would design it to stand as a shell.

I had my doubts about whether our speculative vision would actually materialize. News stories at the time—this was 2014—detailed a trend of instant Chinese towns remaining vacant for years after construction. Often set in areas outside older cities to decrease population pressures, many included towering high-rises, shopping centers, and replicas of European landmarks. According to Eduard Kögel, an urban planner who focuses on Chinese cities, this rapid, large-scale redevelopment "was and is a gigantic, unique experiment."[4] To accommodate the hundreds of millions of people the Chinese government plans to urbanize in coming years, "cities and extensions get built purely based on speculation, but not on direct demand. Massive stretches are built, and it is assumed that the future growth and prosperity will somehow fill the space."[5] The product of a national "build it and they will come" attitude, developers erect new towns as if the final phases of construction were just interim periods, with residents eventually guaranteed to arrive.

Thanks to government intervention, those residents are beginning to appear.[6] Zhengdong, a fifty-eight-square-mile district built around the existing city of Zhengzhou, was once dubbed China's largest ghost town. In 2010, Britain's Daily Mail described the area as plagued by "entire blocks of totally empty accommodation." In 2013, 60 Minutes highlighted it as "a 'ghost city' of new towers with no residents, desolate condos and vacant subdivisions uninhabited for miles and miles and miles." Over time, however, more people have moved in. The construction of a 4.2-square-mile education zone, complete with several government-organized university campuses, has drawn new residents. Recent surveys of the city cite a population of hundreds of thousands of students and staff.[7]

Sparking population growth through government action is an increasingly common move in modern China. Many new towns stand empty for a few years or a decade until the Communist Party convinces businesses, like a new branch of a university, to move to the area. Additional benefits, such as free transport or low rents, often sweeten the city's allure. Tianducheng, China's version of Paris, complete with a replica Eiffel Tower, was plagued by empty streets for years after its construction, but since 2015, the number of residents has more than tripled.[8]

Yet in some cases, cities stay empty. Shanghai's Holland Village, a Dutch-style development, is still dominated by deserted storefronts. The writer of a 2018 Slate article about the area described meeting "an elderly woman who lived inside the town's wooden windmill—the previous tenant, a wedding photography studio, had left it in her care after business went

Tianducheng, China, with its replica of the Eiffel Tower (2018).

south."⁹ Kangbashi, a town initiated in Inner Mongolia over a decade ago, is home today to roughly 10 percent of its originally intended population.¹⁰ China is building husks of cities at breakneck speeds. Some become inhabited; some don't.

I debated raising these issues to the principal in charge of my team but ultimately lost my nerve. I was a low-level worker, uncomfortable telling a man with forty years of experience that his new-town effort could be similarly doomed. I sat down with my colleagues and started drawing instead. Hunched over computers and tables in our California office, we traced arcing lines over maps of topography on the other side of the world, crossing out small dirt paths and modest farm plots to make way for kayak-racing watercourses and waterfall-lined promenades. We left vacant rectangles for apartment buildings that might one day be built and drew in four-lane thoroughfares for high-speed buses. We terraced land to build waterways from scratch, edged with plazas and glass-walled luxury stores.

Kangbashi, a subdivision of Ordos, Inner Mongolia, U. Phalgun (2013).

We were designing for people in a country where many of us had never been, grading hillsides that we would likely never see, displacing families whose names we'd never know.

———————————

Using seductive renderings and idealistic talking points to sell the future as a knowable, happy place—as my Chinese project did—obscures the fact that cities are inherently dynamic ecosystems.[11] In the words of economist Paul Romer, "The urban environment that humans are so busily creating is many things: a biological environment, a social environment, a built environment, a market environment, a business environment, and a polit-ical environment. It includes not only the versions of these environments that exist inside a single city, but also those that are emerging from the interaction between cities."[12] Just like wetlands or forests, cities are the sum of nuanced ties between inhabitants, materials, energy, space, and time. Yet many projects shy away from emphasizing these complex dynamics, focusing instead on visions of tidy towns and clear blue skies.

Rising economic inequality complicates already convoluted conditions, with the phenomenon of ghost cities often making issues worse.[13] Wealthier Chinese citizens often buy ghost-city properties as investments, with little intention of ever moving in.[14] Wade Shepard, author of *Ghost Cities of China,* found that 80 percent of new homes in China are pre-sold, sometimes years before buildings are actually complete.[15] While the rich are able to treat empty cities as long-term investments and live elsewhere until circumstances shift, poorer residents have less choice. In new towns like the one on which I worked, families are relocated to zones where public life has yet to begin.

Yet the complexity of today's cities falls beyond predictive ability. Uber, FaceTime, and Zoom are replacing face-to-face interaction and travel in entirely new ways. Online shopping threatens to make physical commercial spaces obsolete. Many of the world's largest cities are home to more than twenty-five million people and counting, creating denser, more complicated urban environments than the planet has ever seen.[16] As populations grow and climate change accelerates, migration—both voluntary and forced—will skyrocket.

While some cities can densify, there are limits to how fast effective expansion can occur. Building new towns is one way to accommodate the massive urban growth that coming decades will bring. While building instant cities is far from fundamentally bad, most of these efforts prioritize static versions of urban utopias over addressing more complicated urban concerns.[17] New residents might find housing thanks to current explosions of construction. That is no small feat. Yet they will also likely find repetitions of familiar urban issues—substandard infrastructure, social divisions, pollution, political corruption, and so forth.[18] When built as idealized havens, new towns can become tools to bypass rather than address existing difficulties, creating new problems in the process.

As cities grow, existing difficulties become increasingly hard to understand, much less effectively manage. How changes in transportation type, speed, and access might affect economic growth in Tokyo, for example, is a hypothetical question, because cities on that scale have never existed before.[19] Over thirty-eight million people currently live in the Tokyo area—that's half a percent of the entire global population crammed into a few hundred square miles. No single plan is capable of improving the nexus of power grids, wastewater lines, transit flows, economic trajectories, social connections, and resource demands that influence that urban agglomeration, yet traditional masterplans perpetuate the idea that unified visions are up to the task. Mathematical models and analytic strategy can only give an impression of the dynamics at hand. Contrary to frequent claims, negotiating complexity and working with change is the best development can hope to do.

Building cities for static conditions will only become more hazardous in coming decades, not less. Regardless of whether a new town gains residents immediately or grows over time, if it's unable to negotiate shifts in economic patterns, cultural preferences, demographics, and environmental hazards, it will fail. Even new town developments promoted as sustainable eco-cities often don't live up to their branding. Many are simply the same kinds of profit-focused projects pursued for decades, but with new, impressive-sounding names.[20] While new roads, green space, and low carbon emissions are valuable for creating livable environments, few are crafted to negotiate the disruptions that rising temperatures, autonomous transit, and artificial intelligence will bring. Using speculation as a tool for prediction creates urban space that's unable to adapt to modern rates of complexity. Hiding imagination behind calculated rationale leaves cities increasingly vulnerable to twenty-first-century change.

Sense-based modes of working with the future challenge the static confines that characterize so much of modern planning. Feeling into what could be is a reminder that striving to mitigate known risks is no longer enough.

Employing touch, taste, and smell to understand the personal impacts of plans helps us relate to the future as the space of possibility it inherently is. Those personal links are a powerful means of processing, grieving, and working with how aggressively uncertain the future has become.

Superflux harnessed these aspects of our senses to powerful effect with their work on the Future Energy Lab for the UAE. The project invited people to complement analytical awareness about coming decades with a more tactile, emotional understanding. The future, the experiential installation seemed to say, was not a place for logical guarantees, but a field to actively explore, imagine, and feel into what could be.

The project was possible because it had the UAE government's support. Officials envisioned the Future Energy Lab as a means of exploring where the future could and should lead, and shaping energy policy in the process.[21] The effort was one of four labs that the UAE created in the mid-2010s to influence long-term legislation in different sectors. One explored the future of aviation, another the future of blockchain. As its name implied, the Future Energy Lab focused on energy.[22]

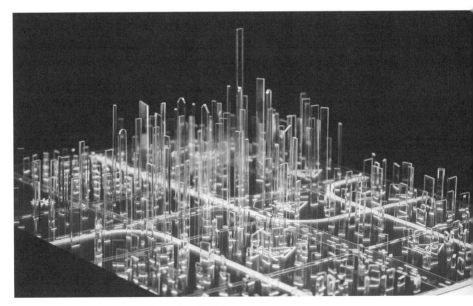

Future Energy Zone model, Superflux (2017).

Government officials wanted to use speculative futures for the effort in part to increase participation. Better collaboration between government sectors and private corporations, previous assessments had pointed out, would be key to transitioning the country from its long-standing fossil-fuel-dependent position to sustained twenty-first-century growth. They needed a space that could invite a range of people to brainstorm what the future of energy in the UAE could become and create policy to make their ideas reality. So they called for help.

Superflux was one of the firms they hired. While another company, Rorosoro, developed an energy simulator and role-playing game for participants to play, Superflux focused on the Future Energy Zone, articulating experiential ways to express the consequences that different energy policies might have on the UAE's environment, economy, and residents.[23]

The pollution machine was one of five different futures Superflux developed. A large model served as a foundation for each. Superflux built a scale version of a future UAE city and then used economic data from the Ministry of Energy to superimpose a range of futures onto the model space. Each one embodied a different scenario of energy implementation, public transit use, energy trading, and cultural attitudes. As participants engaged with different futures, they could assess metrics associated with each one, including a future happiness index, energy-diversification rates, and affordability factors. Changes in costs and carbon emissions produced by each future were also included.

Interactive, design fiction pieces offset the number-heavy experience. They ranged from the noxious air samples to a hologram of a fictional fund advisor designed to help people with payment plans and demonstrate which environmentally thoughtful choices would translate to which types of results. For one scenario, Superflux developed an award—The Order of the Emirates—to recognize particularly enthusiastic environmental stewards and cultivate shifts in cultural attitudes toward climate issues.[24] For another, they made a souvenir of a magnetic levitation (otherwise known as "maglev") train that would connect Abu Dhabi to London. They developed a national grid system based on blockchain technology and created Energycoin as the system's dedicated cryptocurrency.

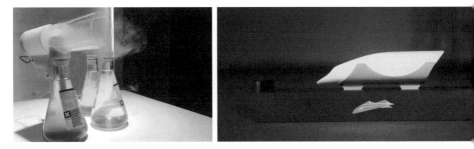

Additional air samples from 2050 (left) and the maglev train souvenir (right). The souvenir model included magnetic tracks, making it functional as well as illustrative, Superflux (2017).

Experiential elements went beyond tactile objects. According to Superflux's website, "participants could track a future happiness index, monitor energy diversification, and observe the affordability and sustainability of each future on an additional screen. They could also observe changes in costs and carbon emissions each of the futures would produce."[25] The firm created the "Tomorrow Fund," a space that encouraged residents to donate to the environmental quality of their children's future lives by making changes in their energy choices today.

Together, the different interactions transformed futures into realities that participants could experience in the moment. In a 2017 TED Talk describing the project, Superflux cofounder Anab Jain explained how one man, after exploring a scenario in which cars were no longer dominant, told her, "I cannot imagine that in the future people will stop driving cars and start using public transport. . . . There's no way I can tell my own son to stop driving his car."[26] Jain responded by handing him the noxious air sample from the pollution machine. "Just one whiff," Jain said, "brought home the point that no amount of data can."[27] Smelling our futures is different from analyzing facts, and creates different modes of understanding as a result. Our senses are avenues that invite deeper connections to ideas, concepts, objects, and experiences. Personal experiences activate different parts of our brains, connecting us to aspects that rational logic can overlook.[28]

Modeling various scenarios and stress-testing them in sensory-based, interactive ways, allowed the Future Energy Lab to integrate analytical insight with personal feeling. The experiential futures encounters surfaced connections between national and neighborhood scales, which in turn helped participants understand links between investment and ecological, social, and technological transformation.[29] Policy decisions became actions with palpable human impact.

The project wasn't perfect. Only a select few were invited to participate, with most hailing from the country's ruling political parties and major businesses. Identified futures developed through the process came from a tiny slice of the country's population. That kind of exclusivity goes hand in hand with working for a government like the UAE. Migrant workers make up over 80 percent of the country's population, and typically lack citizenship rights like subsidized education and health care.[30] Operating in such a country means accepting exclusivity as a given.

Future Energy Zone model, Superflux (2017).

Yet the effort remains a potent example of how feeling into the future directly shapes contemporary choice. Once participants sensed the long-term future they'd prefer, they were able to work back to the present, identifying the policy moves that could lead them toward the desired direction over time. Rather than a predetermined outcome, the future became a destination that people could actively shape.[31]

Focusing on present-day risks over feeling into the future is a development tactic with increasingly serious repercussions. I learned that lesson from my Chinese new town. I helped my team promote the project as ecologically sensitive, a place where blue skies, clean water, and cultural heritage would meld into a sustainable oasis. We would create low-impact development, harvest rainwater, and plant enough new trees, flowers, and shrubs that ambient air quality would improve. Despite the fact that the site is likely to experience serious flooding in coming decades,[32] we graded the town for waterfalls and kayak courses. While recreational pleasure and flood protection are by no means mutually exclusive, flood safety is not always easy to achieve when designs are crafted around fifteen-foot cascades designed for visual effect. Our team shaped some slopes to account for rising water levels and flood conditions, yet paid less attention to how the project sat within its greater region—the steep mountains that surrounded it and the bends of the major river flowing just two and a half miles away.

As I sat in front of my office computer, clicking my mouse to trace lines for new streets, paths, and tiered plazas, I wondered if our plans were enough to prepare the city for coming change. If they weren't, and what we built would be outdated in ten or twenty years, was it really worth the funding, materials, and time required to make it reality?

Today, almost a decade later, advertising declares the city as already finished and ready for visitors. Aerial footage tells a different story. On Google Earth, much of the town still looks like a construction site. Bigger buildings are rising up where smaller structures used to be. The main lake area boasts new waterfall displays, each ranging from seventy to one hundred feet wide. New apartment buildings and villas are rising around the lake edge, with parking lots and pleasure gardens nested in between. A section of four-lane boulevard is graded and paved, with trees planted along adjacent sidewalks and medians. On the other side of the wide thoroughfare, however, containers stand on a construction lot, dispersed in haphazard angles over miles of bare earth. Small shacks and farm plots still occupy the northern edge of the development zone, patchworks of varying green tones and huts with tin roofs arranged along narrow roads. The finished section of the four-lane roadway runs just a few hundred feet to the south, a large-scale future encroaching quickly on the past.

Using speculation to shape a city as if it will handle the same challenges in thirty years as it did at its inception is a dangerous game. If the Chinese new town fills up at the pace my former bosses predicted, it will be 2040 before the population reaches levels it was originally designed to house. By that point, the region is slated to suffer extreme rainfall, flash foods, and rising water tables.[33] The space will still likely do what it was designed for—draw people to the area who would otherwise not have come, and serve as a hub for those looking to spend weekends boating on a lake alongside large, arcing fountains. But will it be able to handle the heavier rains that could inundate the region? Will it weather the impacts of floods regularly hitting the area? Is building shells of entire cities really the only way to house growing populations and foster economic development in years to come?

Projects like the Future Energy Lab demonstrate that embracing our senses helps us do more to imagine and work with coming change. Its specifics are difficult to replicate—the effort was expensive and intentionally designed to cater to select sectors of the UAE's population.[34] It also benefitted from well-funded government support and institutional investment. Those factors can't be re-created everywhere, making the scale of its apparent impact complicated to replicate. Yet we all have the capacity to use our senses—sight, smell, touch, sound, and taste—to personally explore what future conditions could be, refine the realties we want to experience, and craft current-day plans in response.

Feeling into the future motivates us to make more informed decisions today. Speculative futures supports that more proactive, feeling path. The tools create a container to sense what could be and then work back to the present. They help us identify the steps we need to take to make desired futures become real. Developing personal links with what our futures can become helps us articulate and build the world we want to leave, not just to our children or grandchildren, but to the generations who will follow them in kind.

LONG-TERM THINKING

IN THE LATE 2000S, the European Climate Foundation (ECF) made an unusual choice. The international nonprofit wanted to develop a plan to decarbonize Europe's economy by 2050 and needed to find partners to manage the work. It could have taken the typical route of hiring consultants to recommend the most effective and time-efficient moves. It ultimately hired plenty, yet those it chose weren't the kind who focused on mitigating risk. The ECF, a high-profile organization with an eight-figure annual operating budget, funded an effort using speculative futures to shape long-term policy for the entire European Union.

The product was Eneropa. Led by AMO, the research arm of architect Rem Koolhaas's firm, the Office for Metropolitan Architecture (OMA),[1] Eneropa explored what Europe could become if renewable-energy production was the continent's organizing force. It was Europe with the old boundaries dissolved. Spain, Germany, Denmark, and France vanished, replaced by new fictional states molded on the types of renewable energy each could generate. Solaria stretched across Europe's southern, sun-drenched shores, where cities like Barcelona covered rooftops in solar panels. Tidal energy harvesters populated coastlines of gale-prone areas like the UK. Central Europe became Biomassburg, the region's forests interspersed with geothermal plants. Hydropower dams in the Alps formed the basis of the state of Hydropia.[2]

New foundations for statehood transformed existing towns. Under the Eneropa scheme, the German city of Bergheim—currently one of the biggest coal-based energy suppliers in Europe—belonged to wind-farming

states lining the North and Baltic Seas. Its power plants converted to wind turbines accordingly, transitioning neighborhoods long shrouded in thick gray smoke into places with clear skies overhead.

Eneropa was out-there. Getting rid of national boundaries that have existed for hundreds of years, creating a completely new energy system within a few decades, and reshaping the geopolitics of a continent are bold moves. Yet the project received significant funding and political attention.

Eneropa's Tidal States (left) and Hydropia (opposite), Roadmap 2050 (2010).

The ECF underwrote the effort. The *Guardian* called it "a seductive proposition."[3] EU ministers reviewed the findings. How did such an extreme speculative future, presented in full outlandish fashion, get such a serious response?

I discovered Eneropa while sitting on a concrete bench in Honolulu. It was 2018, and I was in town for a few days, working with a local university to help administrators strategize new plans for their campus. Like many institutions of higher education, the university was suffering from the twin evils of dwindling funding and rising dropout rates. Finding ways to use the physical campus to keep the system running had become the administrators' driving goal.

The project was one of my first jobs in a new professional track. I left traditional urban design soon after the new town effort in China, searching for work that didn't lead so directly to community displacement. I worked on responses to sea-level rise in coastal Louisiana. I helped companies construct more energy-efficient buildings. I made the living room from 2200 and started to discover the field of speculative futures. I filled my free time with internet searches for projects that made coming decades feel immediate. I checked out books with titles like *Speculative Everything*[4] and *Thinking about the Unthinkable.*

I eventually landed at a studio focused on strategic planning. My new firm had worked with the Hawaiian university for years on smaller projects, researching utilization rates of building spaces, and analyzing surveys to understand why students kept leaving. When another studio failed to provide the kind of campus redesign they were looking for, university leaders called us.

My bosses wanted to base all design choices on a cohesive long-term strategy. If campus changes were going to support the school over the next twenty to thirty years, administrators had to take a deeper look at what those decades could look like. Given looming shifts in transportation, the new parking garage that some officials wanted maybe wasn't the best use of money. Studying emerging trends, my bosses offered, could identify moves to improve existing problems in ways that set the university up for longer-term success.

The university was open to the idea, but only if long-term meant relatively soon. Ten to fifteen years was feasible. Exploring beyond that, they insisted, was too distant to be useful. When our team tried to convince officials that a longer time horizon could make them better prepared for accelerating climatic changes and technological shifts, administrators demurred.

We sat in one meeting with them for hours, making our case in a dark-paneled room. The space was air conditioned to 65°F, a cold contrast to the balmy Hawaiian day outside. We sat around a wide, wooden table, hands folded in our laps. One of the lead administrators, a slight woman with a blunt bob, sighed as we spoke. Thinking big was great, she said when we finished, but it could wait until later in the planning process. She needed to make sure there was enough funding for the next five years to keep operations running. Looking farther ahead could happen farther down the road. For now, finding the actionable choices she needed meant staying close to the present. Recognizing that it was time to back off, my boss smiled his agreement and wrapped up the session.

I grabbed my bag and followed the group out of the room, thinking about the gentle no we'd just received. The administrator's hesitancy made sense. She wanted to make sure the work we did would result in moves for manageable change. She wanted reliable solutions. I wanted to nudge her toward a more creative place. Finding an example of a big organization using longer time frames, I thought, might open her eyes.

I pushed through the building's double front door onto a paved path, the day's heat sizzling after so many hours in the cold of the meeting room. The rustle of a nearby stream drowned out the bird calls from the trees overhead. The concrete bench stood opposite a stretch of grass. I walked across the lawn, sat down, and opened a browser on my laptop, typing in the words *speculative, planning,* and *long-term.*

Eneropa was one of the first results. While obviously fanciful, the vision was also based on detailed research. A team including the consulting behemoth McKinsey, Imperial College London, and Oxford Economics had worked on the first phase, creating a technical economic analysis of energy rates, greenhouse-gas emissions, and infrastructure conditions across Europe. Results showed that the EU as a whole—this was 2010, years before Brexit—was the world's third largest greenhouse-gas producer and pursued sustainable-energy initiatives in haphazard ways. Huge solar farms stood in the darkest parts of Germany. Wind farms attempted to operate in regions of Italy with little wind.

The research was an argument for a comprehensive overhaul of the power sector.[5] So AMO, the project lead, devised an alternative world to explore what that overhaul could be. Their design explorations transformed the EU into Eneropa, an energy-connected entity built on the facts that the south gets a lot of sun and that wind dominates the north.[6] A centralized grid linked the new states, redistributing power across the continent according to season. In the winter, energy came from strong winds and tidal power states in the north. Come summer, solar power from southern states produced the majority.

Map of Eneropa, Roadmap 2050 (2010).

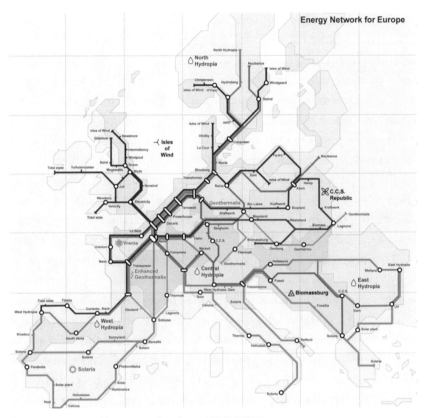

Eneropa energy grid concept, Roadmap 2050 (2010).

It was a whole-scale redesign of the entire continent. While project partners advocated for 40 percent renewables with a large nuclear power component, AMO was more aggressive, pushing for a scheme in which 100 percent of all used energy came from renewable sources. The goal depended on importing power from the Mediterranean's African coast, which could generate more solar than Europe alone. The remaining power that Europe didn't buy, project leaders proposed, could be used for desalinating water and agriculture efforts, boosting economic and social impacts across the North African region as well. The cost would be huge—an estimated six trillion US dollars by 2050—and would create conditions for the continent to become almost entirely energy-independent, with carbon emissions dropping 80 percent from 1990s levels.

Despite its layers of research, Eneropa was never intended as a viable plan. It was a tool to reassess what short-term energy goals for the EU could look like. Instead of providing a concrete destination, Eneropa asked: "If we're going to realize the massive reductions in carbon emissions that we need to achieve in 40 years, what should we do now?" It was a speculative means for finding plausible pathways to attain an ambitious aim.

It was also a way to spark interest, discussion, and collaboration.[7] For the AMO team, using top-down speculative visions had value if the visions could inspire bigger goals. Focusing more on potential solutions than resulting geopolitical issues could, they believed, bring more people together. Before assessing all the obvious reasons why it wouldn't work, they threw Eneropa into public discourse as a "Why not?" and let conversations move from there.

Debate spread. Eneropa's outlandish speculative future provoked growing discussion about the technical and economic feasibility of achieving rapid, large-scale reductions. It was covered by international media outlets, promoted in TED Talks, and talked up in halls of parliament. Commitment to decarbonization has grown across Europe in the years since, with policy implications on internal energy markets and trading systems tied not to the specifics of the Eneropa proposal, but to the emissions goals it helped to shape. The alternative future contextualized long-term goals in a provocative way, inspiring new ways of defining the EU's immediate power needs.

Speculative futures reorients city-making by balancing short-term needs with long-term thinking. Looking beyond today's problems is hard. The present consumes our attention because it's what's in front of us. It's what we see when we go outside, what we feel when we wait too long for public transit during morning commutes, what we smell when air quality deteriorates. It's why urban planning and development are so often reactive types of work. Projects that respond to issues we can see and taste and hear are the ones that motivate us most.

This reactive dynamic creates a particular kind of tension. Building buildings, reconfiguring transit systems, and shaping open space are projects that take years, if not decades, to enact. Most are inherently long-term endeavors, but they're often shaped by present-day concerns. Why pay to repair aging sewer infrastructure when city workers' pensions need to be paid now? Balancing short-term demands with the uncertainties of long-term change is the fraught dance that shapes what urban life becomes.

Friction between long-term issues and short-term concerns is a foundation of how we think.[8] Psychologist and economist Daniel Kahneman details the dynamic in his 2011 book *Thinking Fast and Slow.* Eschewing the phrases *short-term* and *long-term* for the more scientific terms of System 1 and System 2, he describes short-term thought—a.k.a. System 1—as our instinctual brain in action. This is the part of us that knows to flinch when we get too close to fire, helps us avoid speeding cars when we step off the curb, and reminds us how to read subtle social cues during a date. It's through these kinds of direct experiences that we learn to navigate the world.

System 2, long-term thinking, is more conceptual and deliberate. It's the basis for our logical reasoning, our abilities to think in the abstract. In Kahneman's words, it's the part of our brains that "search memory to identify a surprising sound, . . . count the occurrences of the letter a in a page of text, fill out a tax form, . . . or check the validity of a complex logical argument." System 2 is the thought process that helps us plan our yearly spending budgets, complete math problems, and conduct cost–benefit analyses. It's more orderly and, for many of us, takes more effort.

Neither is more powerful than the other. Because System 2 is less essential to our basic survival, however, we often place more emphasis on System 1, our short-term brain. When we go through a risky episode firsthand, we're more likely to reduce the risk of it happening again. It's why people are more likely to buy flood insurance after they've experienced a flood. Because we're the most motivated to act after we experience an event ourselves, we typically engage only after the worst has happened.

That retroactive approach doesn't work today. Trying to plan for events that we've never seen before—and that will happen at some unknown point in the future—goes against our fundamental design. Yet if we don't do that planning, we'll find ourselves in increasingly dangerous conditions. Because issues like climate change are snowball situations—for example, the more greenhouse-gas emissions we put into the atmosphere now will result in increasingly drastic and unpredictable consequences in the future—adaptation and mitigation options demand more long-term thinking. Once we emit those greenhouse gases, we can't simply extract them from our atmosphere or oceans. The laws of physics don't work that way. But because the potential consequences of runaway emissions are difficult to envision, it becomes a topic that's all too easy to delay until a later date.

Proactive planning depends on cultivating more of System 2, on balancing short-term concerns with long-term thinking. As Kahneman explains, "System 1 uses association and metaphor to produce a quick and dirty draft of reality, which System 2 draws on to arrive at explicit beliefs and reasoned choices. System 1 proposes, System 2 disposes."[9] Yet System 2 can also tire easily. It needs motivation from our short-term, System 1 brains. By developing strategies that balance more deliberate, long-term thinking with intuitive, short-term thought, we have a chance of creating actionable plans that adapt to accelerating change.

The tools of speculative futures help us think long-term by making the future feel immediate. When we find ways to connect to events and impacts that we've yet to personally experience, our levels of empathy and engagement grow.[10] Relating to phenomena outside our personal experiences happens when we see a powerful documentary, read a gripping book, or listen to good podcasts. Some speculative futures efforts, like the 1990s movie *Waterworld*—in which all the world's ice caps have melted, and oceans flood whole continents—take more doomsday-based approaches to cultivate interest in long-term change. Others rely on virtual and augmented reality, video game scenarios, or science fiction shorts. The method matters less than the result. When we're gripped by a good story about the future, no matter how it's made, we start to care more. Thinking beyond the envelope of our own lives helps us take the bigger picture more intimately to heart.

Eneropa was a good story. It was a future where the European Union becomes a functioning team, a diverse entity with specific roles designed to support each other rather than compete. By building on in-depth research, it maintained enough realistic ties to make its worldbuilding a tool for assessment and reflection. Being led by a firm with the professional clout of Rem Koolhaas's AMO gave it immediate sway. Its tongue-in-cheek title cased its extreme ideas in humor. That playfulness provided a fun narrative for people to latch on to, cultivating new scales of public interest in exploring strategic long-term change.

The project drew as much anger as interest. Criticisms focused on the fact that it glorified a dangerously simple fix for the union's nuanced energy and political concerns. Architectural history professor Daniel Barber wrote

Eneropa's proposal to bring solar power generated in North Africa to European continent, Roadmap 2050 (2010).

a 2013 opinion piece interrogating Eneropa's wholesale embrace of tech-focused solutions.[11] To Barber, the project suggested "that in order for *the [EU's] social fabric to remain intact,* dramatic changes are needed in *techno-scientific relations to the natural world.*" Eschewing "the larger social and cultural opportunities," and "opting instead for technological solutions that claim little relevance to social change," Barber insisted, is not enough. Rather than attempting to do the harder work of shifting cultural attitudes toward resource consumption and extractive finances, Eneropa did what many development projects have long tried to do—it relied on technological innovation as the answer to complex problems.

It's a valid critique. Eneropa was able to propose such dramatic renewable energy rates largely by importing solar power from North Africa. It's a solution that could theoretically work, but only if the long-standing political, economic, and cultural tensions between the two regions were addressed. Rather than articulating ways of doing so, Eneropa vaguely gestured toward the potential benefit of a massive geopolitical organization of two continents, with little reference to the complex political factors and socio-economic inequalities at play.

Glossing over social and political dynamics in favor of tech-heavy schemes is a tactic that many urban design projects take. Like Howard and his Garden City, the temptation to design entire cities based on the logic of a single individual is the same hubristic drive that motivates people to recreate entire continents. In many ways, Eneropa was the precursor to Bjarke Ingels's Masterplanet project. A unified supergrid for Europe isn't far from a unified masterplan for the entire world.

Yet the designers responsible for Eneropa made a critical choice in how they used speculative futures tools. Where Howard presented his Garden City as a logical solution to nineteenth-century urban ills, and Ingels insists that planetary issues of sustainability would benefit from his single visionary scheme, Eneropa's makers used worldbuilding to provoke public dialogue and debate. Rather than an idealized, achievable utopia, they presented the venture more along the lines of "What do you think about this out-there idea?"

By sharing Eneropa in an intentionally unrealistic way, AMO built the value of the proposal on its capacity to provoke. It was not a project to take at face value. That Europe would abolish all borders and create states with names like Geothermalia was intentionally far-fetched. Instead, the project's silliness was its way to garner interest. AMO employed worldbuilding to point out the ridiculousness of the way Europe's renewable energy grid is currently run. They used humor to highlight the absurdity of investing in solar plants in regions where skies are mostly overcast. As a result, sites primed for introducing new renewable energy projects could be more easily identified, as were opportunities for gaining multiple benefits from new infrastructural development.

The tactic worked. Laura Baird, the project director, noted in an interview that AMO's proposals were "taken more seriously" than anyone anticipated.[12]

Eneropa's Geothermalia (2010), Roadmap 2050 (2010).

AMO used extreme forms of speculative futures to guide long-term energy policy for a continent. It harnessed humor to get an international governing body to think long-term. Even though the final product was a report—a nonbinding recommendation for potential action, to which the EU has yet to commit—the effort undeniably encouraged risk-averse people to explore approaches typically too alarming to even consider.

My firm failed to convince our university clients in Hawaii to take such an open-minded stance. From the start, the administrators were certain that they already knew what they needed—a framework to help them guide campus development over the next ten to fifteen years. They needed to decide whether to prioritize more parking spaces to accommodate existing demand or to invest in better public transit. They needed to determine if reinvesting in the dorms that so many students seemed willing to leave was better than using them in different ways. They knew they needed to promote more environmentally friendly energy plans and improve physical gathering spaces on site. They just needed us to help them prioritize which move to make and when.

I made a small attempt to repeat the argument to get them to think longer-term. I wrote out notes about how more provocative speculation could make their plans more effective. I shared the Eneropa project with my boss, pointing out how its humorous vision of the future helped cultivate a longer-term strategic outlook, that taking a similar tact in Honolulu could provide similar benefits. Focusing on fixing HVAC systems and enhancing campus entryways was valuable. But was it as valuable as thinking through financial models that could handle the drastic funding cuts that could happen over the next twenty years? Was augmenting classroom space more important than understanding the bigger trajectories of remote learning?

My boss looked at me with a slightly sad smile. It was an interesting case study. He'd like to know more. But he needed to move on to another meeting, so how about shelving it for now? He'd already tried to convince the administrators once, back in that cold, wood-paneled meeting room. It hadn't gone well then. It wasn't likely to work a second time.

His disinterest was a faint echo of our client's, an insistence that long-term visioning was a valuable but less crucial aim. The administrators had made it clear that if they were going to look toward the future, it had to be done in ways that would help them get permit approval and funding today. Using forward-thinking speculation to assess the moves that could set them up for longer-term success wasn't essential to reaching those goals. Being provocative presented too much potential for sparking complex conversations they would rather avoid. The arguments our firm made weren't convincing enough to shift their thinking.

The vision we ultimately helped the university make repackaged prevailing concerns into a proposal with innocuous appeal. The campus would become a laboratory for living and learning. Open spaces would be designed to enhance the area's natural landscape and provide opportunities for hands-on education. We used speculation to maintain our client's support. Challenging them to think beyond what they had already convinced themselves they had to do wasn't up for discussion.

Yet speculative futures offers tools for doing much more. By looking past today's issues, they marry the confines of existing worries with the creative thinking capable of handling the disruptions of long-term change. Embracing them empowers us to question our existing assumptions and reinvent the status quo. Eneropa wasn't an attempt to make the most realistic version of the future. It was a future that sparked surprise, conversation, and debate. It helped people integrate longer-term concerns with present-day needs. It provided a vision of what could be so that citizens could brainstorm both what they would prefer in response and iterate ways to get there. Within Eneropa's storylines, humor became a space to balance the demands of today with the changes tomorrow is slated to bring.

Challenging ourselves to look beyond the confines of the present is what equips us to navigate future change. Using humor and play as foundations of design make working with uncertainty more inviting. Provoking creative thought helps us see beyond existing concerns to balance long-term issues with short-term needs. While expert research teams can help the process, they're not essential. Each of us can link our imaginations with our knowledge of the places where we live to start exploring what can be.

SHARED LANGUAGE

IT'S AN EARLY morning in 2070, and you're walking down one of your neighborhood streets. Apartments stack on top of each other into the sky, making the block you're on feel like a narrow alley. The ground beneath you gives a slight spring with each step—energy capture pods are embedded in its surface, adding your kinetic energy to the local grid. In the corner of your eye, you see a few small robots rebuilding a broken window, crawling like spiders as they lift fallen pieces and print new glass on-site. Trees lining the street are still lit up from the night, their leaves embedded with bioluminescent bacteria that make them glow in the brightening dawn.

The street is part of a world you could enter if you wanted to, a world I spent 2019 and 2020 helping to build. A video game designed as an educational program for engineers, it was a dive into what dense urban environments could be like in fifty years. With a virtual-reality headset over your eyes and a set of motion controllers in your hands, you could explore buildings, construction methods, and transit systems as they might exist half a century from now.

Designing a virtual world that far into the future called for using speculative futures full-time. That was new for me. For years, speculative practice was something I did during off hours. I made the living room from 2200 during small slices of the morning and late at night. I looked for examples of speculative design projects online before I went to bed.

After failing to convince the university administrators in Hawaii to think longer-term, I dug deeper into the field. I researched the data-driven methods military strategists often use for futures thinking.[1] I read studies on how sensory perception can foster personal connections to potential change.[2] When I'd share findings with my boss to see if we could incorporate some of the tactics, he was consistent in his reply: creative speculation was interesting, but it wasn't what most of our clients wanted. We were a strategic planning firm. We sold reliable strategies. Imagination wasn't a promised part of the deal.

I started planning my departure. I wrote short science fiction for companies looking for innovative product strategies. I led science fiction prototyping workshops at conferences. And then, in the fall of 2019, I found a studio focused on worldbuilding. They needed someone to lead research on what urban life in 2070 could be like. Did I want the job?

I did. The firm was a mix of Hollywood production designers, product developers, graphic specialists, fiction writers, and computer engineers. I was the only trained urban designer on the team. Working alongside visual artists and 3D animators, I read articles about everything from the conductive properties of graphite to how scientists are using synthetic biology to create self-constructing structures.[3] I interviewed experts for hours in video meetings and translated findings to colleagues in groups chats. We brainstormed details of what 2070 could be during morning check-ins, through late-night emails, and over coffee breaks in the sun.

We built the future city based on questions that might sound outlandish today but could potentially become reality in half a century. The video game was designed for engineers to use, so we focused our inquiries on their kinds of concerns. Asking, "What if buildings could build themselves?" or "What if cities were material banks, able to produce all resources required for construction on-site?" became the future city's foundation.

Each question dictated how I would look for scientific articles or frame conversations with experts during interviews. The questions shaped the workshops we held with scientists, economists, community organizers, and epidemiologists, each collaborator coming from a different background to brainstorm potential answers. Answers led to new questions that, layer by layer, made the city a more high-resolution place.

As the months passed, the video game grew into a world where players could move across time. Depending on interest, the world could shift to 2070, back to 2045, and up to 2070 again. The time scale changes illustrated how roads transformed in orientation, how neighborhoods densified and shrank, how open spaces expanded. You could stay at the regional scale if you wanted, tracing how the city had initially formed along a river. You could zoom instead into different districts, exploring how one zone differed from the next.

Most of the details emerged at the street level. The materials buildings were made from, the kinds of automated pods people used to move around, the ways buildings reused water, and how power was generated onsite—all that was found on the ground. As you strolled down walkways, sat under shade structures, and watched people wearing pandemic-protective clothing, callouts would pop up, explaining how everything worked. You could find out that the shade structures were embedded with sensors that harvested ambient sunlight. You could learn how much energy they generated over the course of the day and how they fed into local power systems. You could learn by feeling into what life in the city was like.

Telling stories about fictional people in a potential future made collaboration in the present possible. Though members of our team had wildly different skillsets, priorities, and frames of reference, we could all relate to the experience of walking down the street. Translating large-scale systems into intimate human stories allowed us to debate, iterate, and refine ideas despite the contrasts in our professional backgrounds. Exploring how shifts in energy generation, transportation, construction, and communication shaped the contours of daily life gave us the language to bridge our divides.

Narrative became a tool to synthesize seemly disparate strains of research. Regardless of how out-there a line of study might seem—systems that transmit solar power from space, for example, or building materials that can grow themselves—we asked how it might translate into contexts where mundane life continued. People will always need food, water, and shelter. We will always crave connection, respect, love, and new experiences. What kind of transit systems and waste configurations would allow us to spend our free time looking for romantic partners in fifty years?

Investigating the kinds of energy grids that could power a dense city in safe, carbon-neutral ways went hand-in-hand with understanding how those grids would impact what residents saw when they left their homes each day. Writing fiction about people's regular lives helped us integrate different research areas, tying them to the range of experiences that residents living in different neighborhoods might have as a result. Those experiences informed not just the physical design of the future city but the ways we talked about the city among ourselves.

One story short I wrote tracked a thirty-something woman as she headed to work. I named her Vilal, a gender-neutral sounding name because research indicated that in half a century, gender might be less culturally important to people than it is today.[4] An engineer employed by the future city administration, Vilal had her own apartment, a rarity in a dense city where personal space was so expensive. Most people had co-living arrangements with family, friends, or acquaintances, but she got hers through connections at her job. As Vilal walked into her living room from her sleeping nook, her furniture reconfigured according to her morning preferences—footstool alongside her favorite chair, window blinds rolled up.

A fast dresser with a rapid morning routine, Vilal left the house quickly. Her building was on a pedestrian side street in a mostly residential area, so the foot traffic outside wasn't too dense; mostly people dropping kids off at corner care centers, taking robot pets for walks, or going to neighborhood fabrication labs to check on what systems needed to be updated and resized for maintenance. Breakfast was a cup of printed proteins from a stall at the end of her block. A lot of the food megacity residents ate was powdered—it was more sustainable and cost less to print repurposed granules than to grow new whole foods. If Vilal ate whole foods, it was usually for a special lunch or dinner, hardly ever for breakfast.

She ate as she walked the couple of blocks to her job. She could have linked in from home—augmented reality made remote working easy—but management demanded a few days of face-to-face interaction each month, and today was one of her in-person days. That morning she focused on transit flows, monitoring where people coalesced through the district, how seamlessly morning commutes were going, whether people grouped in new parts of town. Like most engineers, her training combined studies in coding and structural integrity with subjects like anthropology and sociology. The blend was designed with the hope of ensuring the AI algorithms running the city had as few unintended consequences as possible.

The Vilal story isn't great fiction, but writing a great story wasn't the goal. The point was to integrate research about the future city's large-scale systems into a human narrative. Research provided a sketch of big-picture systems. Each written section translated that big picture into human-scale experience. The responsive aspects of Vilal's living space were inspired by conversations with neurobiologists researching how intelligent sensors could lead to environments that react to personal preferences. That most of the people outside Vilal's apartment were taking care of family members or heading to neighborhood fabrication labs was an idea inspired by different researchers. With the increasingly small size and affordability of tools like 3D printers, fabrication could become more integral to community systems. Rather than paid jobs, many of which will likely become automated over time, work could be tied to maintaining neighborhoods using tools and materials at local fabrication spaces. The hybrid nature of Vilal's work was shaped by conversations with architects, engineers, and planners, who advocated for future engineers with expertise across science, ethics, and technology. Placing equal emphasis on sociological and technical training, they suggested, could help ensure that the people managing artificially intelligent systems would have the interdisciplinary insight that could mitigate the more nefarious social impacts—perpetuating racist stereotypes, for example[5]—of generated algorithms.

Our research provided a big picture of the systems that could sustain cities in coming decades. Our narratives connected the big picture to daily life. While somewhat similar to the "user journeys"[6] many design disciplines employ to align projects with the needs and preferences of those who use them, our approach went a bit further. The narratives weren't meant to craft how people moved through the city. They were tools to see the city through the eyes of its fictional inhabitants. They connected energy infrastructure to the needs of its tens of millions of residents who dream about going on vacation and eating tasty food. They investigated transit systems through the priorities of communities from different neighborhoods, each with distinct goals, challenges, and systems of support.

Using human-centered stories enabled our team—made of people from a range of disciplines and professional experience—to shape the city together. The stories didn't apologize for the width of streets or the placement of power transmission lines or try to sell their value. They didn't romanticize designs for waste streams as the perfect ways to make the city run. Instead, the stories—and the game as a whole—were tools to explore the thoughts and feelings of the people living within. That exploration provided room to think through what could be changed, adapted, or—hope against hope—improved. It wasn't about finding the "right" solution to the problem of how to house tens of millions of people in one urban expanse. It was about trying to feel what living in a future time might genuinely feel like and share ideas for how we might prefer to feel in those future spaces instead. Telling detailed stories about potential futures linked us to language we could share.

Collaborating across disciplines, backgrounds, and expertise isn't always typical in urban development. Improving infrastructural efficiency or securing returns on investment are far more frequent aims. Enhancing quality of life can be a valuable result of built work, something many professionals strive to achieve, yet it's not frequently the go-to foundation of how cities are made. Projects more often begin with surveys of site conditions and environmental hazards than collaboration with those who live or work in the area targeted for change. When collaboration does occur, many teams aren't prepared for the time and effort it requires, leading to problematic results.

This dynamic played out in extreme form in Toronto in the late 2010s. The Canadian city put out a call in 2017 for an "innovation and funding partner" to help redevelop a former industrial waterfront area. The targeted district, Quayside, was a prime location for new housing and commercial space, and many firms submitted proposals for the job. Waterfront Toronto, the government agency in charge, spearheaded selection. When Sidewalk Labs—Google's urban design–focused spin-off—committed $50 million to lead the effort, Waterfront Toronto welcomed its help.[7]

An offshoot of one of the world's biggest tech companies, Sidewalk had vested interest in pushing digital technology in Quayside's design. Indeed, exploring ways to integrate technology into urban space was Sidewalk's founding purpose. The organization was, as its CEO, Daniel Doctoroff, explained in a 2016 blog post, born to "reimagin[e] cities from the internet up."[8] The Toronto project was an opportunity for Sidewalk to test its tech-focused goals at the neighborhood scale.

Nearly two years after partnering with Toronto, Sidewalk finally shared its Quayside plan. It was a study in smart-city tech. The twelve-acre plot remained focused on housing, as the initial call had requested, yet it was housing specifically designed to measure and track the lives of its inhabitants. New mixed-use buildings wouldn't just be built from cheaper, eco-friendly mass timber to make them more sustainable and affordable. They would incorporate high-tech sensors as well. Sensors were embedded throughout the district, from the walls of buildings to streetlights to the asphalt on the ground.[9] Pavement would be powered to melt snow on walkways people used the most. Packages would be delivered by robot. Shuttles and cars would drive themselves. Quayside would be a micro-city made from data-gathering tech, capable of tracking everything from traffic congestion to greenhouse-gas emissions to the levels of trash in trashcans.

Within a year of the proposal's release, the entire project was dead. Doctoroff released a post on *Medium* in May of 2020, declaring that COVID-19's economic impact had made the effort impossible to continue. "It has become too difficult," he wrote, "to make the 12-acre project financially viable without sacrificing core parts of the plan." Sidewalk Labs's leaders painted the end as an unfortunate result of an unforeseen pandemic.

To those who had been following the project, its downfall was the product of a troubled start. The effort was blanketed in secrecy from the beginning, so much so that mistrust between the American tech behemoth and Toronto residents skyrocketed. According to a 2018 profile in *CityLab,* "The founding agreement between Sidewalk Labs and Waterfront Toronto, the government-appointed nonprofit responsible for stewarding the public land in question, went undisclosed until public outcry forced its release."[10] Sidewalk tried to calm the tensions by opening a community space for engagement and publicly talking through residents' concerns, yet conflict only continued to rise.

Fears spread that Sidewalk Labs's promises of a better urban future masked its deeper goals of selling software and monetizing personal data. When asked to address those concerns, Sidewalk's explanations remained vague, its officials unwilling to share specific details. Local activists protested Quayside's progression as a result, arguing that Sidewalk Labs's data-gathering methods could easily create a real-life version of George Orwell's *Nineteen Eighty-Four.* Bianca Wylie, an open-governance advocate and critic of the project, wrote a December 2017 opinion piece in Canada's *Globe and Mail,* arguing that "smart cities are largely an invention of the private sector—an effort to create a market within government. . . . The business opportunities are clear. The risks inherent to residents, less so."[11] Almost a year after work on Quayside began, Sidewalk Labs had still shared little about how the data collected would be owned and used.

The project quickly transformed into political suicide. According to a piece by writer Sidney Fussell in *The Atlantic,* one former advisor and privacy expert quit Quayside after becoming concerned that Google would use collected data to augment its proprietary algorithms.[12] Once Sidewalk finally published its design intentions for the site, Waterfront Toronto Chairman Stephen Diamond actively distanced himself from the master plan, declaring in an open letter that he and his group "did not co-create" the plan, and that Waterfront Toronto and Sidewalk Labs had "very different perspectives about what [was] required for success."[13] Toronto was left with little option but to derail the project entirely.

Making technological solutions the foundation of its designs left Sidewalk ignorant to residents' actual desires. Self-driving cars, its plan insisted, were necessary today. Trashcans that documented what people threw away and when were deemed essential. Rather than working with residents to identify technological tools they wanted to use, Sidewalk assumed new tech and big data was the answer. Instead of taking the time to explain how data collection and processing would operate, Sidewalk glossed over the demands of the very populace the project claimed to serve. "How are they so bad at this?" local opinion pieces asked.[14]

Sidewalk's tech-focused attitude is increasingly common in modern planning. Ben Green explores the growing trend in *The Smart Enough City,* writing that smart tools are often used as simple fixes to avoid "making political decisions that involve complex trade-offs and that could engender legitimate differences of opinion." Installing automated streetlights and driverless cars can seem more straightforward than fixing aging public transit systems, making smart cities an attractive prospect. Objective, data-based answers to technical problems offer less contentious cover.

Pushing urban-focused technologies has accordingly become a go-to answer for solving urban problems around the world. The allure has led to what Green calls "tech goggles"—"the perspective that every ailment of urban life is a technology problem that only technology can solve."[15] Improving traffic issues, accident rates, and energy efficiency just by installing a few new tools is a premise that can appear too seductive to ignore.

Sidewalk used tech-goggle blinders to sell a future to people who didn't want what they were selling.[16] By not taking the time to create trust and a shared vision with Toronto's residents, it paved over the human impacts of the work it proposed to do and set the stage for its own demise. Toronto residents pushed back because the story Sidewalk tried to tell about the future of their city wasn't one they supported. Instead of collaborators, Torontonians were treated as bystanders with needs that came secondary to Sidewalk's tech-focused agenda. It was a project with little common language built or shared.

Toronto has pushed plans for Quayside forward in the years since the Sidewalk project dissolved. A group of developers are leading a new scheme for the site[17] that includes hundreds of affordable housing units, a "community forest" of car-free open spaces, and "Canada's first all-electric, zero-carbon master plan."[18] While the exact role that sensors and other digital tools will play in the development is unclear, city officials insist that engagement with local communities and other stakeholders will be an ongoing part of the process.

Yet engagement doesn't always mean collaboration. As the next stage of the Quayside story unfolds, I find myself wondering whether involved professionals will treat city residents more like co-designers or spectators. Will they invest in the time and tools it takes to build a common vision? What would a shared language for Quayside be like?

Lack of civic collaboration is no longer an option in how we build our cities. When residents aren't involved, proposed projects often die, as Sidewalk's scheme for Quayside did. If they're built, they come with higher risks of enacting changes that don't work for the people who live within. No single plan, no matter how visionary or steeped in research, will create strictly positive impacts over time. Exploring potential repercussions is just as important as investigating possible solutions. Iterating on alternatives is often fertile ground for collaboration to grow. Yet collaboration can't happen unless those involved have language they can share.

Speculative futures facilitates communication by centering human stories. Not everyone feels empowered to create detailed visions of new developments in their cities, but we can all imagine the kinds of changes we want to see in the neighborhoods where we live. Working with the power of those stories lays the groundwork for real collaboration to occur, collaboration that can build the social resilience that today's challenges demand.

That truth was palpable on the future city video game I helped to create. Worldbuilding allowed us to facilitate scales of collaboration that I had never achieved in previous urban design projects. Our team was able to work with people from economics, community organizing, blockchain tech, renewable energy, and more because we used stories to find common ground. Words like *risk* had very different meanings for engineers and economists. We bridged those gaps by making the lives of the people and communities inside the future city the basis for conversation. Beginning the project by asking questions—What happens if the city is not just carbon neutral but carbon negative?—created spaces for people to work together by orienting within their own understanding and areas of expertise.[19] In doing so, the worldbuilding process supported a shared language from the start.

Moving between scales in the project, both in space and time, helped ensure that the human story stayed centered. When we addressed conceptual issues like modular construction techniques,[20] we asked how their use might shape pedestrian pathways. We wanted to know how they would impact apartment size and function over time. We invented characters and neighborhood traits to guide design, making sure streets, storefronts, transit systems, and power grids reflected how residents got up in the morning, what they did for work, and how they relaxed. We explored long-term change by encouraging players, collaborators, and participants to feel into the real-world impacts of what they were seeing. When we discussed how retrofits of lower-density districts might be done, we made sure to explore how construction could be made quieter for residents nearby.

More detail led to better collaboration. Toward the beginning of the project, when our designs were rougher and our understanding of the city was just starting to take shape, we didn't have as much to show. Ideas and feedback were more general as a result. "What about space for aerial vehicles?" one engineer asked when we showed her a sketch of downtown streets with a dense tree canopy. That same engineer, presented with a later rendering of a rooftop charging space for aerial transit and delivery units, started detailing the kinds of electric transistors it could use. This back-and-forth in the worldbuilding space allowed us to reflect on proposed designs together, to assess how realistic they were, what issues arose, and what needed to be changed to better accommodate those involved.

The game's interface was designed to reinforce that feedback loop. Programmers created elaborate commenting systems so that players could leave questions, thoughts, and concerns as they moved through the virtual city, and brainstorm potential solutions as well. Rather than enacting direct change, the idea was to provoke new trains of thought that could address both the long-term impacts of projects built today and problems that could soon emerge.

The commenting system got to the heart of the video game's intent— it was made to spark conversation. Like films, books, and other narrative forms of speculation, it offered an alternative vision of what could be to provoke different kinds of thinking about potential futures. How successful it was in doing so is hard to know. Measuring shifts in perception about possible trajectories is difficult at best, and the game is currently still in beta form. Real-world developments might one day be shaped by its designs and narratives, but that's far from guaranteed.

What is certain is that the worldbuilding space supported interdisciplinary and cross-cultural collaboration. It allowed our wide-ranging team to communicate across professional and social gaps, because it wasn't striving for a singular outcome. It made room for questions until the questions outlined a story with shape, nuance, and scale.

Better collaboration is the gift that speculative tools like worldbuilding can offer. They're forums for shared language to take root and grow. Few know how to construct electrical grids or build the foundations of multi-story structures, but everyone can articulate how they want to use power in their own homes. Worldbuilding acts as a framework for development that isn't about asking residents to share their thoughts on existing designs, but about giving people the tools to advocate for the spaces in which they hope to live. Finding shared language helps us imagine and build the futures we want.

BEYOND INCLUSION

SEARCHING THE DEPTHS of Vimeo one night, I found a short depicting the future of South Los Angeles.[1] Set sometime in the 2030s, it followed a Black woman with a British accent exploring the neighborhood of Leimert Park. Solar panels stretched across building rooftops and slow-moving autonomous cars cruised the streets. Shade canopies over street-level garden plots were drum-activated, pulling back to let in the sun when people began to play. When the woman walked down a sidewalk edged with citrus trees and herbs, a text box popped across her augmented-reality glasses, telling her she was welcome to take what she liked—the plants were grown for people passing by. Another pop-up declared the autonomous cars were free to use. When one slowed down, the woman got inside, where she was immersed in audio about the neighborhood's landmarks and historic sites, like clubs where James Brown and other musical legends used to play.

The short, I soon learned, was part of a project called Sankofa City. An effort led by Leimert Park residents and University of Southern California (USC) students, it used speculative futures tools to envision the future of the neighborhood, with community members acting as the primary designers. Their efforts explored a single, complex question—how could a future where emerging technologies like augmented reality and self-driving cars were commonplace also support a vibrant and empowered community?

It was the kind of project I'd spent months trying to find. This was December of 2019, early in my time working on the future city video game. As thrilled as I was to be paid to shape urban environments with speculative futures, I was creating a product primarily for engineers. At that point, my living room from 2200 installation was one of the few pieces I'd encountered that made detailed visions of potential worlds available in public spaces for wider groups, and it was my vision of the future that the installation had shared. I'd found the Columbusplein project a few years prior, which emphasized community collaboration, and the Candy Chang–inspired sidewalk chalk project before that. A collection of other projects had emerged in the time since, but they were far from the majority.

Still from *Sankofa City,* K. Baumann (2017).

Who was using speculative futures as planning tools to cocreate what the future could be? I spent nights and afternoon breaks from work filling internet browsers with grammatically fractured phrases like "speculative community planning" or "speculative futures visioning community." My searches yielded results on everything from definitions of what community visioning is to meetups for people interested in urban activism. The occasional projects I found that used speculative futures focused mostly on their value in improving interdisciplinary research or enhancing the efficacy of community meetings. Powerful goals, but they didn't aim for the degrees of collaboration I was hoping for.

Stills from *Sankofa City,* K. Baumann (2017).

That night, reflected in the blue light of my computer screen, I found a different kind of approach. Sankofa City not only used speculation for community-based planning but made the visions of the Leimert Park community the basis of the planning process itself. Rather than coming up with isolated ideas of how tech could act as a community asset, project leaders and residents worked together to find the answers.

Sankofa City is urban planning that goes beyond inclusion. It's a goal that many development projects have yet to explore. Inclusivity and participation have been central rallying cries ever since writers and activists like Jane Jacobs started advocating for community-based development in the 1950s and 1960s.[2] With each passing year, more academics and practitioners call for "place-based" knowledge and "participatory, adaptable, and responsive planning."[3] It's now widely acknowledged that planning can't continue to prioritize the visions of privileged groups. Aiming for inclusion has become an accepted way to ensure that past exclusions stay in the past.

Yet inclusion has real limits. Most importantly, it sets up a binary approach to planning—people are either included or left out. Those included have to operate within systems made to further the interests of a select few.[4] In countries like the US, architecture and planning have been shaped by Eurocentric frameworks of what constitutes good urban space. Planning as a distinct profession began to emerge only in the 1800s, as a reaction to the increasingly crowded conditions and public health concerns of industrializing cities.[5] The first academic planning program popped up at the University of Liverpool in 1908.[6] Harvard followed with its own program, the first in the US, in 1923.[7] The men who developed these programs and laid the groundwork for the discipline to grow were white, informed by European ideals of what cities should be.[8]

Because their reference points are still steeped in European influence, much of today's westernized planning systems reinforce values associated with whiteness. Those values have created planning cultures more often focused on perceived "dysfunctions" in communities of color, than on inequalities propagated by planning systems themselves.[9] It's a dynamic tacitly designed to perpetuate racialized economic inequality, resulting in drastically different degrees of social resilience from one community to another.

For communities that aren't white, working with and within these systems is an old and continuing struggle.[10] When the Supreme Court ruled that zoning laws targeting Black Americans were unconstitutional in 1917,[11] local governments created new, less overtly racist tactics. Provisions like banning multifamily developments and setting standards for minimum lot sizes spread across the US, driving up the cost of housing beyond levels many non-white families could afford. The practice of redlining, in which neighborhoods were color-coded to allow or deny mortgages to prospective home buyers, accelerated in the 1930s. Neighborhoods with majority Black populations were identified as "red areas," where federally secured loans were systemically denied.[12] The 1950s and 1960s saw the acceleration of urban renewal, which gutted so many Black neighborhoods to make way for highways and commercial developments that writer James Baldwin called it "negro removal."[13] Modern-day urban renewal efforts often redevelop urban spaces in ways that make property values spike, displacing existing residents in the process.[14] As neighborhoods of color are frequently the site of such projects, the burden of displacement is skewed. For those able to stay, health problems are common, as formerly redlined neighborhoods tend to have more environmental issues, such as higher concentrations of harmful air pollution.[15] That urban-development fields are still largely white places compounds these problems. Over one hundred thousand architects are currently licensed in the US. Just two percent are Black. Of all those awarded degrees in the fields of urban, community, and regional planning, over half are white.[16]

Designing for inclusion begs the question of what systems people are participating in, what standards of value participation requires, and who sets the standards to begin with. So while talk of making planning more inclusive is growing, there is less talk, and much less consensus, about the fact that encouraging people to engage in systems that aren't designed to put their interests first is problematic and dangerous both.

Given this context, more designers—mostly people of color—are starting to insist that aiming for inclusion in urban development is not enough. Amanda Williams, a Black architect, told the *New York Times* in March 2021 that "the word inclusion makes my skin crawl. . . . It implies tolerance: tolerating Black people, tolerating a monolithic idea of Blackness."[17] Dimeji Onafuwa, an adjunct professor of design, gave his own take on the topic in an interview a few months prior, explaining that the promise of "inclusion" toward marginalized communities is based on a process of convincing people to engage with the systems and spaces that excluded and marginalized them in the first place.[18]

Avoiding the pitfalls of inclusion is difficult for even the most well-intentioned projects to achieve. Take what happened in Oakland, CA, in 2020. Across the bay from San Francisco, Oakland is a city that prides itself on being progressive. It's the kind of city where suing the federal government is common, where new mayors ride to their inaugurations in Burning Man art cars. In the early months of the COVID pandemic, Oakland tried to continue that progressive trend by expanding its Slow Streets program—an initiative to make streets safer for walking and bicycling by closing them to traffic.

I watched the work unfold during quarantine in my home in neighboring Berkeley, tracking changes from my laptop. In short order, the city installed barriers on twenty-one miles of streets, creating a network for outdoor social distancing. The barriers were small—mostly traffic cones and temporary signs. Placards signaled that deliveries and emergency vehicles could still pass through, in addition to residents getting to and from their homes. The idea was to reclaim space from cars when many people were largely housebound, ameliorating feelings of pandemic isolation and re-envisioning what the city's streets could be in the process.[19]

Initial surveys sent out to evaluate residents' responses received some glowing reviews. In May, one commenter said a Slow Streets corridor in their North Oakland neighborhood had made a real difference to their daily exercise routine. "It has been wonderful to run in a safe space where it is very easy to practice social distancing and not worry about dodging other pedestrians and risk obstructing or being hit by traffic," they wrote. "I really appreciate this initiative!" Another resident focused on the benefits of fewer cars. "We have less traffic in the neighborhood and I like that from a safety standpoint. Second, there's more sense of community with neighbors and an overall feeling of safety. Less cars also means less noise pollution and air pollution. Big plus!"[20]

Yet Oakland city planners leading the project noticed a glaring issue. Most of those positive responses came from people living in North Oakland, an area populated by wealthier residents. Many living in that region could telecommute for work. Many were white. Many of the proposed Slow Streets, however, were in predominantly Black and Brown communities in East Oakland, where COVID was hitting hardest. Many residents in those areas were both essential workers and members of some of Oakland's poorest communities. Having more walking space on streets was much less important for them than being able to pay rent, get safely to and from work, and not catch COVID.

East Oakland residents were far less happy about the new program. One survey responder, highlighted by the *Oaklandside*'s coverage of the issue, had no time for the closures and their unintended consequences.[21] "The combination of closures with no enforcement has simply made our streets *more dangerous*, not less!!!" they wrote on the public comment board. "Autos still use this as a 'through' street; they still speed, now at even higher speeds!! The 'barriers' are not stopping traffic, and in fact, traffic now goes into oncoming, speeding autos!" Others stated they would have rather had the city focus on fixing the long-standing problem of potholes before starting the program, if only to make the streets safer for bicyclists and newcomers to the area.

That the city rolled out Slow Streets with little public notice made tensions worse. An article in *Oakland Voices* explored the planning process behind the effort, explaining that the idea of closing streets to through traffic had already been introduced in a 2019 city-approved plan to install neighborhood bike routes.[22] Associated initiatives to install traffic diverters, speed bumps, and other measures were in different stages of execution in the winter of 2019 and 2020. When the pandemic hit, many planners saw a valuable chance to expand the existing work.

They weren't wrong. Large-scale disruptions like COVID are reminders that the status quo can quickly change. But that approach—seeing disruption as opportunity—is positive only when all affected residents are part of deciding what capitalizing on opportunity means. It's that aspect of collaboration that's too often ignored. Writer Alissa Walker cited the issue in Curbed in the early months of COVID, pointing out that many—mostly white—urbanists were framing the pandemic as an "opportunity to accelerate their pre-pandemic agendas—agendas which ignore the issues that made COVID-19 more catastrophic than it should have been."[23] Oakland did what many have done—got excited about the potential for change and pushed forward without meaningfully working with the communities those changes would impact the most.

Slow Streets was waylaid, in part, by its own ambition. As media outlets like Next City noted, the city failed to adequately address the mistrust neighborhoods of color have when it comes to the planning department.[24] John Jones III told an Oakland Voices reporter that scores of residents viewed Slow Streets as another tool for displacement.[25] "Oakland has a long history of decisions being made by the City that adversely affect communities," Jones said. "How information is shared with the community is problematic. 'Shelter in place' and 'Come and exercise in the streets' is a conflicting message." Slow Streets were not the answer East Oakland residents were looking for. If anything, they wanted helped getting to places like grocery stores and clinics.

Luckily, Slow Streets was made from temporary interventions that could quickly adapt to feedback, and local communities were organized enough to make their voices heard. When residents pushed back, pointing out that the program did little to really address the problems COVID-19 was causing them, city planners listened. They slowed the program and created more avenues for public review. Rather than continuing to implement closures citywide, they adopted a pop-up, request-based approach, creating interventions more likely to build on what people actually needed rather than what planners thought they wanted.

They also introduced a new program to help residents access neighborhood services. Called "Essential Places," it used a mix of the temporary traffic interventions that Slow Streets had employed—like cones and signs—to slow traffic and make intersections safer, helping people get to grocery stores, food-distribution sites, and COVID testing facilities.[26] A COVID-19 information hub provided multilingual placards with information about testing locations, housing support, and other amenities.[27] Feedback on the program was largely positive. Even those still wary of Slow Streets noted the benefits of navigating formerly hazardous intersections with a little more ease.

I know some of the Oakland officials who worked on the Slow Streets effort. They're caring, considerate professionals who want to help the city's communities grow stronger. Yet those same communities had to work hard to make their serious concerns heard. Getting excited by an idea and persuading others to accept it is a difficult legacy to let go, even for the most well-meaning people.

Tracking the project from my laptop at home, I wondered what would have happened if city planners had started by asking community members what they needed. Instead of inviting people to weigh in on a program that was already developed, the city could have started the conversation with a question, something like "What do you need to survive?"

———————————

Hundreds of miles south and over a year prior to Oakland's efforts, Sankofa City used "What do you need to survive?" as its north star. Sankofa project leaders were talking about gentrification rather than COVID, but the stakes were similar. Decimation and erasure threatened both communities.

Sankofa answered the question by using speculative futures. Initiated by Leimert Park residents and students from USC's department of cinematic arts, the Sankofa work built on years of collaboration between the school and the neighborhood. Throughout the 2010s, students and community leaders had been running workshops to explore how aging urban objects like payphones, newspaper boxes, and benches at bus stops could be reimagined to strengthen local identity. The workshops started largely as a response to plans for a transit line that would connect Leimert Park to Los Angeles International Airport and downtown Los Angeles. That transit line was poised to bring more people to the neighborhood and exacerbate rates of gentri-fication already changing the area. Rather than let gentrification accelerate unchallenged, local residents wanted to see how creative collaboration and placemaking could strengthen the neighborhood's sense of identity and build cultural connections that new arrivals could understand and embrace.[28] Sankofa City's workshops built on that history of collaboration as a next step.

The goal, according to Karl Baumann, a former USC doctoral student and one of the project's leaders, was to spark public conversations about "what alternative futures look like, particularly when they're tied to local culture."[29] What role did people want new technology, for example, to play in their lives? What would everyday life look like once augmented-reality glasses or autonomous vehicles were widespread? What might happen if the neighborhood had its own self-sustaining gardens?

Conversations took place in more interactive versions of community planning meetings. Participants from a range of backgrounds, including tech, fine art, music, engineering, and design, came together for workshops over the course of fifteen weeks. Rather than simply asking participants to identify lists of desired improvements or to comment on already proposed developments, the Sankofa project asked people to imagine themselves in 2030. This kind of role-play turned the workshops into an experiential futures space, where people could imagine what sounds they might hear, what smells would be around, what the air might taste like, and how they might spend their time in coming decades.

Urban researcher Matthew Jordan Miller attended the Sankofa work-shops and wrote about the experience for the *Journal of Planning Theory and Practice*.[30] The imaginative role-playing, he said, "not only intensified the quality of our separate interventions, but it increased our interest col-lectively. Each team's characters began to talk across the modes and imag-ine how their protagonists might find it exciting or difficult to exist in that world." Instead of using local feedback to shape urban space, the Sankofa project used worldbuilding and speculative design to reimagine what shap-ing space actually means. "We were literally building a new set of narrative-driven worlds," Miller wrote, "through placemaking." Serious play became an opening to shape new futures.

Sankofa City workshops extended over fifteen weeks, K. Baumann (2017).

Sankofa City concept diagram, K. Baumann (2017).

As the workshops progressed, participants started playing with the idea of their neighborhood becoming not just a future version of Leimert Park, but another kind of place entirely—Sankofa City. The Sankofa Bird is part of West African symbology, a being that creates vibrant futures by linking the past with what lies ahead. Sankofa City, they decided, would mix that Sankofa Bird spirit with the culture of Leimert Park. It would have some primary values, like community-based policing, gardening as a tool for placemaking, complementary autonomous cars built and designed by local shops, and publicly accessible augmented-reality projections that shared stories of local history. With each session, participants deepened those ideas through design fictions, by building toys, props, digital models, and, eventually, the film short I found years later on Vimeo.

The project introduced more nuanced shifts in attitude about the role technology might play in coming years. Factors that outsiders might have viewed as problems became space to explore potential opportunities. Drum circles, which some new residents in the neighborhood consider noisy disturbances, were reframed as civic tools to manage solar-power systems. Local teens, often seen as disruptive or dangerous, were hired to help build the district's fleet of autonomous cars, giving them valuable civic roles as well as jobs. It offered a vision where gentrification wasn't a given, but one of many possible trajectories.

The work became a blueprint for community desires, made to guide discussions on how the future of the neighborhood could evolve. The visions cultivated in Sankofa City gave residents more cohesive ideas of how they wanted Leimert Park to transform, as well as more agency in advocating for their preferences. The final presentation, made to a community stakeholder group, was a forum for dialogue about long-term strategies to integrate new technologies in the neighborhood and strengthen its identity over time.

Not everyone at the final review was immediately supportive. Some stakeholders were skeptical, unsure about why proposed innovations were necessary. Why, a few wanted to know, did they need autonomous cars? Because Sankofa City was developed with a range of community residents, including people from professional-design backgrounds, the presenters were ready to assuage concerns. When a reviewer questioned whether neighborhood youths could actually help fabricate autonomous vehicles, a

Autonomous vehicle prototype in a Sankofa City workshop (left) and in the video short (right), K. Baumann (2017).

teammate who worked as a transportation engineer stepped in to confirm that they indeed could.[31] Because the teammate was both one of the co-designers of the proposal and connected to the community, his comments landed. By the end, reviewers said they were "inspired" by the process and excited to build on its findings.[32]

For now, that building is focused on creating free autonomous shuttles for the neighborhood.[33] Ben Caldwell, a longtime Leimert Park resident and one of the co-leaders of the project, is spearheading the initial pilot tests to see how a larger fleet could be introduced over time.[34] Thanks to the Sankofa City video, he has more local support for this next phase of the work. While autonomous cars initially struck some as an unnecessary addition, the speculative short helped to ground the idea in the reality of daily life. If autonomous shuttles were free, the short suggested, that might be a valuable community use. Watching the idea play out in narrative form got people motivated and on board.[35]

Still from *Sankofa City,* K. Baumann (2017).

That USC students and Leimert Park residents used speculative futures to collaborate resulted in a narrative rooted in place. When the stories being told belong to us, when they come from our own lives and reflect what it means to live in our communities, we're inherently more connected to what those stories show. We can push generated ideas more effectively to the next level of impact as a result. It's why storytelling is key to cultivating sustained investment in proposed plans. It's why speculative futures can help enact city-making systems that go beyond inclusion. Rather than acting as the "experts" in the room, professional designers and planners can use speculative tools to welcome residents as co-designers. Rather than feeling pushed aside, residents and interested parties can use the power of their own imaginations to cultivate ideas that work for them and advocate for their needs accordingly.

By using collective imagination to shape urban space, Sankofa City offers an alternative model for development, one that invests in collective, community-based imagination about what could be. Slow Streets had to evolve into Essential Places because the city of Oakland tried to push for measurable outcomes too quickly. What would have happened if each had combined elements of the other? What if Oakland had asked its residents, particularly those who view the planning department with deep suspicion, to help them envision what they wanted their streets to become from the start? What if Sankofa City was able to link its visions directly to city-supported implementation? What if the process of collaboratively imagining future conditions happened on an ongoing basis, so that when drastic events like a pandemic occur, cities would have community-supported responses ready to go?

Any community is capable of doing what Leimert Park did. Whether through writing stories, playacting future scenes, or building models out of clay, everyone has the capacity to envision the futures they most desire. Once those futures take shape, it's up to us to make them real.

COLLECTIVE
IMAGINATION

MIDWAY THROUGH 2020, I woke up to orange skies. It was an early September day, and my alarm rang at its usual time. Yet when I opened my eyes, the world stayed dark, more like midnight than morning. I pulled back the curtains, and an orange glow filtered inside, turning the walls of my room into a brooding pumpkin. Outside, the streetlights were still shining. What was going on?

A half hour online provided some answers. Wildfires had been raging across California since the middle of August, burning homes and people and cloaking the region in smoke for weeks. Local air-quality agencies explained that strong winds had temporarily moved the smoke and ash to higher elevations. The debris blocked out the blue light from the sun (the shorter wavelengths), letting only yellow, orange, and red rays (the longer wavelengths) to pass through, giving the Bay Area's skies their new color. In areas where the smoke was particularly thick, even yellow rays were blocked, painting the world a haunted crimson.

The orange sky ironically brought better air quality than the Bay Area had seen in weeks. Since the wildfires began, the air around San

Francisco—normally clear and fresh from ocean winds—had become the worst on the planet. So many fires were burning around the state, and at such a ferocious pace, that going outside had become a toxic activity. Public health organizations advised staying indoors and taping plastic sheeting over windows to keep out the smoke. When the world turned orange, however, that toxicity lessened. With most of the smoke higher in the atmosphere, the air at ground level was left cold and relatively safe to breathe. The world was suddenly a place where the day was dark, and apocalyptic skies meant it was finally safe to walk without air-filtration masks.

Familiar scenes of street corners and front yards were newly unnerving in the orange glow. I explored my neighborhood in a daze, occasionally taking a photo to send to friends and family in other parts of the world. "It looks like the new *Blade Runner!*" one of them wrote back. The sequel to the 1982 sci-fi classic, the film is set in 2049, in a world of climate-ravaged cities and orange-tinged skies. Residents live in alone in tech-supported apartments or decaying buildings, masks covering their tired, weather-worn faces whenever they step outside.

Midday in Berkeley, CA, on September 9, 2020, as wildfire smoke turns skies orange.

My friend was right—walking the neighborhood did feel like the movie. At noon, streetlights were still blinking through auburn haze. Car headlights wavered on smoke-tinged air. Coffee bars and noodle shops sat boarded up to abide by pandemic shut-down orders. Like me, other residents moved slowly through the streets, their faces warped with disbelieving frowns, incredulous that a sci-fi Armageddon had become real life.

The *Blade Runner* films aren't alone in their dark depictions of what the future might become. Most sci-fi visions of the future lean dystopian. Steven Spielberg's *AI* is set in a flooded New York City devastated by climate change. Spike Jonze's *Her* dives into the social isolation that could stem from pervasive automation and artificial intelligence. In less well-known sci-fi works, like 2015's *Gold Fame Citrus*,[1] social and environmental collapse spur people to escape cities entirely. In *Woman on the Edge of Time* (1976) and *World Made by Hand* (2008),[2] nonurban spaces are the only areas where human life can flourish.

These dystopian visions of the future already influence the ways cities are made. Architect Adrian Smith has said his ideas for Dubai's Burj Khalifa, currently the tallest structure in the world, came from seeing the *Wizard of Oz* and its Emerald City as a kid.[3] The biometric scanning and three-dimensional mobility depicted in *Minority Report* are rapidly becoming urban reality across the globe. In many ways, the dance between dystopian speculation and city-making is a "the chicken or the egg" situation. Did *Minority Report* inspire the personalized advertising and touch-screen technologies we have today, or would we have developed them without the vision of the film? It's impossible to know.

It's also impossible to deny that images of alternative worlds haven't impacted the people designing our products, infrastructure, and cities. This has been true for generations. Ebenezer Howard's nineteenth-century visions of the Garden City were heavily shaped by science fiction and fantasy, specifically Edward Bellamy's *Looking Backward: 2000–1887*.[4] The book, which envisions Boston in the year 2000 as a socialist utopia, was the third largest bestseller of its time, after *Uncle Tom's Cabin* and *Ben-Hur*. Inspired by its descriptions of peaceful streets, green trees, and orderly stores, Howard wrote *To-morrow: A Peaceful Path to Real Reform* in 1898, detailing his visions for the Garden City's suburban ideal. Those plans, according to urbanists like Lewis Mumford, did "more than any other single book to guide the modern town planning movement and to alter its objectives," toward the urban-renewal craze that dominated so much of twentieth-century development.[5] Howard's vision of separated urban and suburban life was a speculative future shaped by someone else's imagination. And

Burj Khalifa, D. Tong (2012).

while his Garden City was influenced by utopian fantasy, its results led to negative impacts that affect cities even today. It's a real-life echo of the Hieronymus Bosch painting "The Garden of Earthly Delights," a triptych depicting the fall of utopian dreams into devastation and decay. Idealistic fantasy can easily turn dark through single-minded translation.

Speculative fiction and sci-fi stories aren't just made to explore where we could go in years to come—they're commentaries on the prevailing cultures of the times in which they're made. Orwell's *Nineteen Eighty-Four* proved eerily prescient in predicting our current surveillance-focused societies, but he wrote the book to explore themes of government overreach and totalitarianism in the Soviet Union and 1940s wartime Britain. The 1927 Fritz Lang film *Metropolis* was conceived as a response to the new skyscrapers and rapid growth of New York City in the 1920s, exploring what life could be like if that vertical trend became even more extreme. Its form is now echoed in cities from São Paolo to Shanghai.

City life depicted in Fritz Lang's *Metropolis* (1927).

Hieronymus Bosch, "The Garden of Earthly Delights" (1480–1505).

There's an inherently reciprocal relationship between the speculative worlds we envision and the urban realities we build for ourselves. The original *Blade Runner*—with its dark, narrow streets and teeming nightlife— appeared in the early 1980s, when planners and architects were trying to shift away from the hyper-clean modernism of the previous decades. The movie showed a diverse, cacophonous city, filled with different kinds of fashion and food, where humans and nonhumans walked the streets together. The dark, unequal, and dangerous world it presented was a gritty counterpoint to the status quo, alluring in its difference. Syd Mead, the visual designer who helped craft the *Blade Runner* aesthetic in 1982, often visited the Gulf region before his death in 2019 to consult on new developments.[6] "The Middle East is a fantastic example," he's been quoted as saying, "of how reality is catching up with the future,"[7] where the scope and size of construction are matched only by the speed with which projects are built. The half-century since the Gulf first grew rich from oil coincides with a concerted rise of dystopian urban futures in video games, fiction, and Hollywood films. In that time, cities like Dubai have evolved as echoes of those visions, becoming hubs of towering skyscrapers, buildings that echo exotic animals, and islands terraformed into the shape of palm fronds.[8]

The Shanghai district of Pudong has developed into a dystopian future city made real as well, with raised walkways and buildings hundreds of meters high. A span of paddy fields and factories as recently as the 1990s, the district has transformed into a special economic zone attracting international capital and famous architects. Shining corporate headquarters of companies like Pepsi and Samsung now dominate the skyline. Narrow avenues run between skyscrapers splashed with multi-story ads of attractive women selling snack foods. It's a present-day version of *Blade Runner,* which itself was shaped by director Ridley Scott's interest in Asian architecture. The film's street life was inspired by places like Taipei's crowded Shilin Night Market and Tokyo's neon-filled Shinjuku shopping district.[9] Now those ideas have been fed back to the Chinese ruling class, shaping their ideas about what urbanism should be. A 2013 photo of a Beijing skyscraper shrouded in smog with a video running on one of its facades is an uncanny replica of the dark, perpetually rainy city life depicted in *Blade Runner.*[10]

Still from *Blade Runner* (1982).

The ways we imagine future cities have material impact. Dystopian speculations of the future made decades in the past have become the present. Stephen Graham, a professor focused on cities, technology, and speculative fiction at the University of Newcastle, sees "a really startling and disturbing similarity between a lot of these sci-fi vertical dystopias and the current practice in, say, the Gulf, where the elites inhabit their penthouses and fly around in helicopters and business jets while literally thousands of workers are dying every year to construct these edifices."[11] By shaping our conceptions of not only what is achievable but what might well be inevitable, our collective stories determine the cities and realities we create.

This dystopian dominance is a problem. When existing visions of the future skew so heavily apocalyptic, adaptive planning becomes more difficult to achieve. It's something academics have noted for decades. A 2001 article sounded an early alarm, asking people to consider "the implications of the exploitation, environmental degradation and violence that stalk the cinematic city."[12] More recently, writers like Naomi Klein have warned that the domination of dystopian visions in popular culture has led to widespread views that catastrophe is unavoidable.[13]

When doom and despair are our foundations of what the future will become, proactive action is nearly impossible. While it's likewise problematic to paint the future with a rose-colored brush, looking almost exclusively to dystopia as a guide leaves little room for more creative potential. As writer Jill Lepore recently declared in the *New Yorker,* dystopia has become "the fiction of helplessness and hopelessness. It cannot imagine a better future, and it doesn't ask anyone to bother to make one. . . . Its only admonition is: Despair more."[14] Predicting only unavoidable suffering makes us abandon our agency and accept destruction as inescapable.[15]

More dystopian fiction is hardly necessary to make the future seem bleak. Research and reality are enough. A 2017 article in *New York Magazine* titled "The Uninhabitable Earth" synthesized an array of scientifically feasible worst-case climate trajectories into one scenario. The result was a future of new plagues seeping from melting permafrost, the forced migration of hundreds of millions of people, and droughts and floods as horrendous and frequent norms.[16] My September 2020 walk around the block, my skin orange under the glow of that sinister sky, was scarier than any apocalyptic movie I've ever seen because it was real. What lies ahead if the status quo continues is truly frightening, as dark a vision of the future as any sci-fi dystopia can get.

This is not to say that dystopia isn't valuable. It can be a powerful means of reflecting on and questioning current conditions. Author Paolo Bacigalupi, for example, has focused his writing on asking difficult "what if" questions to explore the effects of climate change on future societies. In one of his latest books, *The Water Knife,* he dives into a near future in which Arizona is gripped by devastating dust-bowl conditions, the Colorado River has been reduced to a trickle of water, and the millions of people who rely on it are in danger. The story was partly inspired by people he met during research trips who believed that because major droughts in the Southwest had never reached catastrophic levels, devastation was unlikely to happen in coming years. Interested in challenging those assumptions, Bacigalupi wrote his book to explore "people who are living on the shards of the future . . . who took a wrong turn and are living with the consequences."[17] His text isn't focused on presenting potential solutions, so much as highlighting the risks of looking to the past to anticipate what could be. It's dystopia as a tool for sounding the alarm.[18]

Yet continually dwelling on fears about the future can make disaster seem inevitable. Researchers find that rather than inspiring preventative or adaptive action, fear makes people want to look away. As psychologist Dolores Albarracín writes in *Action and Inaction in a Social World,* fear is only effective in motivating people to change if the changes required are easy and the stories sparking the fear are not overly frightening.[19] One 2007 study Albarracín ran on HIV prevention and treatment found that fear of AIDS did not make people use condoms or other safety measures during sex. Only counseling and more widespread testing seemed to shift knowledge and behavior over time.[20] Addressing climate-changed futures and navigating the AIDS epidemic share important lessons—scare tactics are too scary. Propositions focusing on impending doom can spread a problematic type of logic and psychology. Looking the worst in the face makes most of us stick our heads in the sand.

Even when dystopian visions of the future incite people to action, working with the feelings of despair that often follow is hard to do. A study surveying the effects of the 2004 film *The Day after Tomorrow,* in which a climate change–induced ice age freezes much of the northern hemisphere, found that while the film was successful in making viewers want to mitigate climate impacts, it failed to help them figure out how to do so. Its outlandish depictions of environmental catastrophe—at one point the lead characters run from an ice freeze as if it were a wild animal and escape by shutting a door against the encroaching cold—also blurred people's abilities to distinguish scientific facts from dramatized fiction. Participants still expressed their desires to take proactive climate action. That's a kind of win. But because the film provided no information on what forms proactive actions could take, a sense of despair followed.[21]

Big change requires belief that change is possible. It requires a kind of collective imagination that allows for the birth of what doesn't yet exist.[22] Polling conducted by the Nature Conservancy found that people are much more likely to get involved in action initiatives when future scenarios are placed in a positive light.[23] Too much dystopia limits motivation, expanding senses of helplessness until despair is all that's left. Defending against a negative option is harder than finding ways to enact a desirable future.[24] Creating visions that people want to move toward rather than run from is an essential part of cultivating proactive adaptation. Starting from a position of optimism and possibility makes taking action a viable choice.

Challenging today's dystopian dominance does not mean that more utopian visions are the answer. Modernism's ideas for utopian cities turned out to be nightmares for those who had to live in them. Instead, exploring a middle ground[25] can push against the hegemony of dystopian narratives without creating false hope in utopian alternatives. Writer Ursula K. Le Guin's 1974 novel, *The Dispossessed: An Ambiguous Utopia,* for example, explores a world in which people put the needs of society ahead of their own. As its subtitle suggests, however, this society is not perfect. Instead, Le Guin offers something much more valuable. By working with the realities of human greed, jealousy, and fear, her fiction becomes a testing ground for exploring the limits of more communal societies and understanding how individual pursuits can support collective well-being. Investigating potential repercussions is just as important as highlighting hypothetical benefits.

Finding balance between the two is not a simple task. When the skies over San Francisco turned dark orange that September 2020 morning, the internet gawked at a dystopia unfolding in real time. "It is LITERALLY *Blade Runner 2049* in California right now," film critic Kevin Lee posted on Twitter.[26] Pop-culture writers showed side-by-side images, asking, "Can you guess which of these is concept art for *Blade Runner 2049* and which is the current San Francisco skyline?"[27] "Nightmarish," people responded.

And it was. 2020, already a year of pandemic lockdowns, death, and political oppression, provided yet more proof that doom wasn't just on its way, but already here.

Other people had different takes. Aneesh Raman, then an economic advisor to California governor Gavin Newsom, took to LinkedIn to push back against the growing cascade of dystopia porn. "Just to be clear," he wrote in a single-sentence tirade, "we'll take the apocalyptic wildfire sky in SF today since the air quality is clean enough for us to open our windows given that we're just out of a historic heat wave and have to conserve electricity so the grid stays operational in part because we're all at home working and learning, while also thinking about systemic racism and the fragility of democracy, as we battle a pandemic." Raman's voice resounded as a level-headed antidote to the alarmed craze, a reminder that, for some people, accepting the worst as a given is not an option.

Still from *Blade Runner 2049* (2017).

By the end of that September day, the orange skies began to disappear. I spent the evening rewatching *Black Panther*. I was designing the future city video game at the time, and the darkness of the orange skies made my feelings about coming decades take a decidedly darker turn. Until that point, the project had been a place of solace. I had started working on it in 2019 and continued throughout 2020, as COVID raged, as racial tensions became more violent in the US, as divisive elections loomed. Amid the mounting uncertainty, the future city had been a forum to look beyond my fears of the present and envision what might happen in years ahead. It was a refuge where I could actively remember that the problems of today aren't necessarily destined to last.

The orange day drained that sense of possibility. I suddenly felt depleted, depressed, and small. If the world could turn so upside down that daylight grew dark, then full apocalypse was likely close behind. I needed some positive visions of where the future could lead. I needed a few hours in a different headspace. So I made some popcorn, poured a drink, and streamed *Black Panther*.

The first scenes of Birnin Zana—the capital of the fictional African kingdom of Wakanda and the home of *Black Panther* superhero T'Challa—came into view ten minutes in. Tall towers twined with dense vegetation. Streets spacious yet busy with market storefronts blended into walkable spaces that still left room for public transit. Timbuktu-style scaffolding and Malian-esque pyramids mingled with high-speed trains and energy-transfer systems.

As I watched, my breathing began to ease. My shoulders unfurled. My growing calm didn't just come from watching T'Challa being a wise and noble kind of superhero, or seeing the female warriors who guarded him kick ass. It came from spending time in a world where renewable energy wasn't a fantasy but a given. It came from diving into a culture that balanced technological innovation with the health of nonhuman species. It was seeing people connect to their cultural traditions and collaborate across their differences. Immersed in Wakanda, the memory of smoke-filled skies

◄ Midday in San Francisco, CA, on September 9, 2020, as wildfire smoke turns skies orange, C. Michel (2020).

and orange Armageddon started to feel less like a death sentence than a serious warning.

When the movie ended two hours later, I wasn't ready to return to the real world. I opened a browser to investigate how the film was made instead. Though Birnin Zana is a high-tech city, Hannah Beachler, the film's production designer, developed it not by diving into its technology but into its people. In an interview with Bloomberg's *CityLab,* she explained that "the people were the most important thing" about her process.[28] She spent months shaping the city's architecture, clothing, food, transportation, and ways of life, amalgamating her research into a visual history and guidebook. Hundreds of pages long, the guidebook served as a kind of bible for the movie and included histories not just for Wakanda's infrastructure and technology but for its diverse populations. She articulated a backstory for how Wakandans mined vibranium, the nearly indestructible element that powers their country. She created a Hall of Records where residents could go to learn about their history.

The Hall of Records was a particularly critical component for Beachler. It was essential, she explained, for "every person in Wakanda to know where they came from,"[29] that theirs was a society built on connection to history, culture, and place. She saw Wakandans as people who "know everything about their past. . . . There's not an African in Wakanda who can't find out who they were, where they came from, for thousands of years." Beachler knew that if the people of this fantastical world had the gift of knowing their ancestry—a privilege that she as an African American woman has not had—they would be more rooted in their values and identity, and stronger as a result. The 2018 megahit and one of the highest-grossing films of all time used worldbuilding to make a city and culture based on people.

Black Panther is an afrofuturistic vision of urban life. Far from a concept invented by production designers like Beachler, afrofuturism has been a growing international movement for decades. Much of Western media has overlooked people of color for centuries, suggesting that the present and future are places where Black, Indigenous, and other peoples of color don't belong. For generations, many writers, musicians, designers, and artists have actively challenged those narratives, articulating instead an endless array of futures where Black people thrive. Musician Sun Ra believed that the future of Black people could be interstellar, a belief that he translated into his music, clothes, and performances. Rather than focusing strictly on the problems Black people were facing at the time—Sun Ra started his career in the 1930s and remained active until his death in the 1990s—he invited people to imagine a different way of being.[30] Octavia Butler's *Lilith's Brood* is technically a postapocalyptic story in which most of humanity is extinct. Yet she, a Black female writer, turned that bleak future into a thoughtful exploration of the role gender and consent can play in rebuilding civilization. Over the decades, afrofuturism has emerged as a way of preserving Black bodies by projecting Black identity, culture, and representation into the future.

Today, afrofuturism is thriving across disciplines, including fine art. A 2016 effort called the Iyapo Repository used design fictions to prototype afrofuturistic realities. Created by Ayodamola Okunseinde and Salome

Image for Sun Ra's album *Space Is the Place* (1972).

Asega, the project was both a museum and resource library housing artifacts that affirm the futures of Black people. Okunseinde and Asega created the space to ask, "What are the objects that Black people will need to thrive in the coming years?" As a Black man, Okunseinde wanted to expand his personal reflections about the future to a wider scale, in the hopes of sparking changed ideas of where the future could lead. Rather than devising the objects themselves, Okunseinde and Asega invited different communities to help them to create drawings of future artifacts. This crowdsourced process drove the effort, offering participants a different access point for envisioning themselves in an increasingly changing world.

Afrofuturism is a reminder that part of challenging dystopian dominance requires looking critically at the people who make the speculative futures we absorb. Articulating what the future can be requires making assertions about wider trajectories of time and how systems will unfold.[31] As Frank Borchardt, a professor of linguistics, noted in *Doomsday Speculation as a Strategy of Persuasion,* many dystopian visions "misrepresent themselves by concealing their presuppositions." Making such decisions without identifying and understanding the worldviews behind them can ultimately present subjective ideas about potential futures as more universal truths.

The majority of future visions in popular culture often come from narrow, privileged groups. The Hugo Awards, one of science fiction's most prestigious prizes, have overwhelmingly gone to white men, who continue to write the majority of science fiction even today.[32] And while utopian sci-fi undeniably exists—hello, Edward Bellamy's *Looking Backward* or Kim Stanley Robinson's *Ministry for the Future*—the vast majority trend dark. Aldous Huxley's *Brave New World,* George Orwell's *Nineteen Eighty-Four,* Ray Bradbury's *Fahrenheit 451*—the list goes on and on. Although women certainly write their fair share of dystopia—Margaret Atwood's *The Handmaid's Tale* is as sinister as it gets—white men create the most. This is true in film as well. Although Marvel movies have been made for nearly two decades, Ryan Coogler, the director of *Black Panther,* is the only Black person to direct a Marvel film thus far. In 2019, just 18 percent of filmmakers in the US film industry were people of color.[33]

Speculative approaches like afrofuturism offer more plural visions of where the future could lead.[34] This is as true for urban planning as it is for filmmaking. The Sankofa City project, for example, used a distinctly afro-futurist foundation to support the visions of Leimert Park's predominantly Black community. From the West African word *Sankofa* to the solar panels activated by drum circles to the thriving Black community that uses augmented reality and driverless cars to celebrate its history and culture, the project harnessed new tools to show how Black people could thrive in coming years.[35] An exploration of what the end of Eurocentric visions of cities might look like, it was a retelling of who gets to shape the spaces we call home.

Black Panther brought afrofuturism to a new level in mainstream culture, offering an alternative take on what urban space can be. Based on the real African empire of Mutapa—a powerful trade center that stretched across present-day Zimbabwe and Zambia from the fifteenth century to the eighteenth—Wakanda's capital of Birnin Zana envisioned what the people of such a nation might have become if they had never been colonized. What, the film asked, would their society look like today?

The result was a future city unlike others typically shown on television and in film. The tall glass towers and master-planned cities so often depicted were nowhere in sight. A more bottom-up, community-based kind of urbanism emerged instead. "If you've ever wondered what kind of innovation and wealth black people could produce," writer Brentin Mock wrote in a 2018 piece for *CityLab*, "had they never been subjected to the decimating forces of colonialism, slavery, lynching, Jim Crow, mass incarceration, second-class citizenship, and racial segregation, Wakanda is it."[36] Streets were populated with busy stores and markets. Buildings looked like residents had retrofitted them over the years to better suit their needs. Roads were made as much for food stands as for transit lanes. Urban space seemed shaped to enhance the quality of residents' lives rather than enact bureaucratic plans. It was a reminder that the number of ways to shape and inhabit cities are endless.[37]

The planning world exploded on Twitter when the film first came out, filling the *Black Panther* hashtag with urban development–focused themes. "No cars," one planner declared, "walkable streets, super-efficient public transit, place-based & culturally sensitive architecture & design at all scales, & I presume no homelessness or poverty—last night's outing to see #BlackPanther had me wanting to meet #Wakanda's chief city planner."[38] Others wanted to know more about the city's rapid-transit system. "I don't really understand how the trains work in terms of where they stop, etc.," someone wrote, "but the pedestrian streets and building density in Wakanda are fantastic!"[39] Some focused more on the economics of the city. "Are the citizens capitalists?" another planner asked. "Are the towers residential? Are they collectively owned condos?"[40] Moving through the world of Birnin Zana offered all the ideals designers often talk about—pedestrian-friendly streets, vibrant commercial centers mixed with public space, green vegetation used as infrastructure and woven throughout city centers—in cohesive, realized detail.

Black Panther still, depicting the city of Birnin Zana (2018).

Perhaps most importantly, the film is based on a non-Western world-view of what cities can and should be. Wakanda is a vision of a different kind of nation, and Birnin Zana is a different kind of city, where a non-white approach to land use and infrastructure is celebrated. As then PhD student C. N. E. Corbin wrote in *Planning Theory and Practice,* "These are urban creations of a different ideology for a different land and for a different culture." They offer an "urban aesthetic grounded in understandings of African cultural productions; shapes, colors, designs, and functions."[41] It's a space where non-Western visions of what urban development can be are the foundation from which urban life grows.

Wakanda's non-Western worldview pushes back against some of the oldest stories about what people are and what we're designed to do. Kendra Pierre-Louis explores this train of thought in her piece "Wakanda Doesn't Have Suburbs."[42] The tale of Adam and Eve, she reminds us, in which the two are kicked out of the Garden of Eden, is another way of saying that humans are designed to ruin the good things given to us, that destroying our environment is to be expected.

The Western worldview, in which destruction is a guarantee, is hard to escape. It's a message many of us have tacitly absorbed over time. In 2013's *Braiding Sweetgrass,* Robin Wall Kimmerer—a plant scientist and member of the Citizen Potawatomi Nation—writes that hundreds of her ecology students declared in a series of surveys that humans and nature are a bad mix. These were people who had chosen to dedicate at least portions of their lives to environmental issues and conservation. "How is it possible," Kimmerer wanted to know, "that in twenty years of education they cannot think of any beneficial relationships between people and the environment?"[43] For every example of people positively engaging with their environment, we internalize far more presenting dystopia as our unavoidable destiny.

Speculative futures helps us challenge that narrative. Using its tools can reorient collective imagination, reshaping dialogues about what cities can be and what urban planning should offer. Ensuring that people from different backgrounds are at the forefront of articulating those futures safeguards against narrow ideals dominating public discourse. *Black Panther* is one of few mainstream examples of what can happen when we tell ourselves different stories. It's an alternative to modern civilization that looks radically different from the sprawling suburbs of the US, the vertical mirrored towers of Dubai, or the high-speed trains of Singapore. It shows how sophisticated technology can support positive relationships between urban residents and their environments. Birnin Zana soundly rejects the idea that humans and ecological systems are inherently at odds.

Black Panther makes me ask what the world could be like if real-world cities did the same. What if we saw ecology and man-made infrastructure as fundamentally connected? What if we were able to see the challenges posed by climate change not as a guaranteed path toward destruction but as incentive to repair what we've broken?

The film does what the best kinds of speculative futures help us do—ask ourselves, "What if?" and "Why not?"

VISION
INTO ACTION

"SO." THE WOMAN GRIMACED as she spoke, dragging out the *o* as if it were a dubious life raft.

I was leading a workshop on using speculative futures in long-term planning, and the session was almost over. Just this question-and-answer phase left to go. For most of the previous hour and a half, the woman had seemed attentive. Her face was one of many in the neat Zoom grid filling my screen, her curly hair bouncing up from her head, her septum pierced with a gold ring glinting just above her smile.

She was frowning now. "We've got our ideas. How do we translate them into action?"

I took a long sip of water, unsure of how to respond. It was the spring of 2021, and the pandemic was still raging. The future city video game project had ended a few months prior, and I'd begun to lead more future-visioning workshops, exploring what people wanted to create in their post-pandemic lives. That day's group, a collection of designers, artists, planners, and city residents, had spent the afternoon working through ideas for how to adapt to climate change over the next thirty years. Some wanted to address mud-slides that could happen in the aftermath of wildfires and came up with schemes for catching earth with terraced jungle gyms. Others devised community-warning systems and pop-up shelter spaces to take care of people fleeing extreme weather.

Their ideas were exciting. I wanted to see all of them realized. But the woman asking the question had zeroed in on the essential issue. Using creative tools to come up with bold visions for the future is great. But once you have a vision, how do you implement it?

———————————

Implementation is city-making's most basic and elusive goal. Building is an obstacle course of codes, zoning, funds, and timing. Costs often balloon beyond budget. Permitting moves at a glacial pace. Enough time might pass between conception and construction that development stalls entirely. If you're part of a community with an idea you want to execute, it's far from guaranteed that idea will come to life.

Projects based on more creative kinds of speculation can be even harder to realize. Most efforts aren't intended to translate into built work at all. *Black Panther*'s non-Western vision of urban life was created as entertainment. Sankofa City was primarily designed to cultivate deeper community collaboration on future development in LA's Leimert Park. The Republic of Columbusplein was initiated to reorient residents' attitudes toward shared public space. Designed as creative, exploratory tests, those efforts were effective in sparking new levels of civic dialogue. None were specifically designed to result in direct, lasting change. To create more resilient cities, however, using speculative futures to identify new visions for city life isn't enough. After we think about what kind of futures we want, many of us want to start to build that future, or at least find out what we can do to begin the process.

Embedding speculative futures tools into planning work translates shared visions about what futures can be into physical reality. Without that connection, even when agreement on a desirable future exists, implementation remains difficult to achieve. The aims of international initiatives like the 2015 Paris Agreement have so far largely stalled because they lack that critical link. According to Joost Vervoort, assistant professor in environmental governance at the Copernicus Institute of Sustainable Development, large-scale international agreements are often successful in setting clear aims, but typically fail to translate the aims into effective action. In the case of the Paris Agreement, the aim was limiting global temperature increases below 2°C by 2100. It was an ambitious and, according to participating scientists and activists, achievable objective. Yet the agreement stopped short of committing to the granular details of what nations, citizens, and policymakers needed to do to realize that future—the where, when, and how of what fulfilling the vision entailed. Subsequent commitments made at the COP26 conference in Glasgow in 2021 provided more specifics on what achieving those agreements entails.[1] Yet with no international framework in place for holding participating nations accountable, there is little real enforcement. Remaining in the realm of vague promises has so far kept the vision from substantially moving beyond an idea of what's possible.[2]

Big transformations depend on access to the motivation, funds, and skills needed to reach identified goals, and monitoring implementation and impacts over time.[3] Developing a cohesive vision is just one piece of the process. Strategy, execution, and dedication make concepts real. Those factors are what planning and development avenues provide. Identifying action steps for a desirable vision—linking creative speculation into planning—provides both motivation and momentum to enact desired change.[4]

Yet building those links is difficult. Reaching out to planning departments takes energy and time. Coordinating community desires with city prerogatives demands a complex balance of municipal management and local grit. Bring in planning officials too early and the risk that institutional objectives will overpower community interests runs high. Get them involved too late and valuable funding, construction, and organizational opportunities might be missed. Sometimes the two can find equilibrium but there's no guarantee.

Projects that effectively translate speculative vision into action often use speculative futures as foundations of development. A striking example began in 2012, in a small community in Ghana. Two architects, D. K. Osseo-Asare and Dr. Yasmine Abbas, began working with residents from a place called Agbogbloshie, a seventy-five acre[5] scrapyard famous for being the place where "data comes to die."[6] Discarded computer pieces, cables, and disk drives from all over the world end up in the area. Thousands of people make their living scrapping from the waste, repurposing circuit boards, transistors, and copper wire for new use.

The concentration of tossed-away tech has created a dangerous environmental situation. The *Guardian* called it "the world's largest e-waste dump" in 2014. *Wired* called it a "hellscape" one year later.[7] Toxic smoke, in particular, is a big part of life in Agbogbloshie, with the burning and soldering it takes to extract valuable materials creating poisonous conditions both for people and the local ecology.

Yet it's also fostered a sophisticated circular economy. Agbogbloshie is home to robust systems of local exchange, with a wide range of recyclers and makers dedicated to giving unwanted parts new life. In residents' skilled hands, cracked refrigerators and broken semiconductors become affordable computers, refurbished cooking pots, and personalized welding torches. As a *Smithsonian* article put it, the scrapping and recycling happening in Agbogbloshie is "an important business that plays a key role in bridging the so-called digital divide between wealthy consumers in developed countries and those in places like Ghana."[8]

Inspired by their abilities, Osseo-Asare and Abbas wanted to find ways to support what locals were already doing. How could design, they wondered, enhance the positive aspects happening on site? How could they—architects from outside the community[9]—use their training to improve conditions in the area? How could they make this complex economic system more physically and environmentally safe? What kind of support did Agbogbloshie residents actually want?

Residents burning wire to recover copper at Agbogbloshie, Accra, Ghana, M. ▶ Chasant (2019).

To answer those questions, Osseo-Asare and Abbas took on the roles of mediators and instigators. They didn't choose plans to move forward or guide residents in particular directions. Instead, they focused on fundraising, sparking conversations, and coalescing ideas into actionable schemes. And they used speculative futures to do it.

The two architects began by spending months around the recycling businesses. They collaborated with local makers to map out where people worked, where different activities took place, where disassembly happened, where scrap pieces were stored. "We collected data about the waste stream," Osseo-Asare explained in a recent piece, "and modeled these flows all the way from the import of products, their reuse, their recycling, and ultimately to their export."[10] As the two got to know more residents, they started to hold meetings and visioning efforts. They hosted workshops and used findings to help people iterate on potential plans. Many Agbogbloshie residents were migrants, they learned, with little education and limited connections in big cities. Making money and making it fast was a widespread need. If Osseo-Asare and Abbas were going to find a way to make conditions safer and environmentally sound, they realized that finances had to be a focus.[11]

Making and resourcefulness in Agbogbloshie. Many residents are expert at rapid prototyping, AMP (2014).

Rounds of meetings and interviews resulted in the "AMP Makers Collective," a group of over 750 local makers and scrap dealers from the Agbogbloshie area. Osseo-Asare and Abbas invited hundreds of students, recent graduates, professionals, and researchers in STEAM[12] fields to join the collective as well. Makers in Agbogbloshie were expert at rapid prototyping, able to make sophisticated samples of desired products quickly, using the basic fabrication tools at their disposal. That facility with making, Osseo-Asare and Abbas reasoned, contrasted with the more theoretical approach many designers use in school and the workplace. The people who design products, spaces, and tools are often not the ones who do the fabrication. Just think of the way big companies like Apple or Microsoft have most of their products constructed in countries like China, rather than in the US, where many of those companies and their designers are based. Facilitating dialogue and collaboration between Agbogbloshie makers and STEAM students became a way to translate skills and information not just from academic spaces to Agbogbloshie, but from Agbogbloshie to the rest of the world.

Over time, the AMP Makers Collective came up with the idea for the Agbogbloshie Makerspace Platform (AMP). A hybrid physical and digital space for crafting, the effort was based on the idea that if recyclers had access to more sophisticated tools and gear, they could make their products in safer ways. So the collective designed and built a platform to serve those needs. The physical space was a prefabricated, solar-powered kiosk for prototyping and building, outfitted with customizable tool kits that could be reconfigured based on what local makers wanted to make. It was modular, making it easy to assemble, disassemble, and assemble again where it was needed, using the tools and workforce readily available in Agbogbloshie.

The digital space was a trading app to link makers to new markets for their goods. It was a logical next move—people make more money when they're connected to wider networks of potential customers. A "mix of Twitter, WhatsApp and Craigslist,"[13] the app was designed to help people generate more steady income, amplifying their existing reputations as makers as well as their potential for long-term growth. It also gave them

Construction on the modular maker space, AMP (2014).

information about how they could better protect themselves from environmental and health hazards. As Osseo-Asare wrote in a 2019 paper, the two aspects served as a "network linking recycling with digital fabrication and distributed manufacturing, as well as (a tool to provide) people with a better understanding of the hazards of certain materials."[14] It was education through economic growth that supported residents to choose what worked for them.

AMP isn't automatically identifiable as a speculative futures effort. It's not set in a distant future or an alternative reality of the present. It's grounded in the needs and logistics of today. Osseo-Asare and Abbas used their skills as designers to help locals articulate their own ideas of how to

Digital app testing, AMP (2016).

create safer, profitable work in their neighborhood. That meant, according to Osseo-Asare, "mapping out an alternative production and health future for the district at large, in collaboration with workers and residents."[15] By envisioning tools to help residents improve their economic security and physical safety, AMP helped people prototype a new future for their community.

Prototype is the operative word here. AMP was a test to find an alternative future for Agbogbloshie. It wasn't developed to convince locals about ideas they should embrace. It wasn't predicting a particular outcome. It used speculation to stretch community members' imaginative muscles of what their work and lives could become. It used speculative futures to ask them, "What if?" and "Why not?" It used worldbuilding to help them shape a vision of the future that they would be interested in building over time, articulating the economic systems that could result in healthier environmental and social conditions. By investing in relationships with resident makers, that mode of provocative speculation encouraged collaboration and iteration that's become a foundation for impactful change.[16]

Once known only as a toxic wasteland, Agbogbloshie is now increasingly seen as what it has been for years—an innovative space for recycling and making. It's rewriting its history to envision and build a different future where African-produced tools enhance existing community capacities and skills. It's a future that builds upon the traditions of creativity and resourcefulness that have shaped the area for generations, weaving positive aspects of the past into the present and future. As Osseo-Asare said in a 2018 interview with *Atlas of the Future*, the work wasn't "just about trying to fix a problem" but focused on "building startups and projects that can be interlinked with" [17] Agbogbloshie as well. Addressing issues of waste and environmental pollution, he insisted, can be opportunities to build skills, grow new modes of employment, and support sustainable businesses.

Not all designers would see that possibility in a place like Agbogbloshie. Not all residents might see it either. Working together, however, recyclers and architects were able to use imagination—a fundamental tool of design—to think provocatively about what could be. Because that provocation was directly embedded in the strategy, planning, and execution of the project—How could we do things differently here?—Osseo-Asare, Abbas, and their collaborators were able to bring a different narrative to life.

I tried to adopt some of Agbogbloshie's collaborative emphasis in my Zoom workshop on speculative futures and long-term planning. Osseo-Asare and Abbas had made facilitation both the root of their work and a goal that residents could demand in more vocal ways. They introduced speculation about the future in forms that emphasized not only the power of collaboration but also the possibilities it presents. In similar fashion, I wanted to explore frameworks that could support people in pushing for the kinds of changes they hoped to enact in their own communities. I'd been refining the workshop for years. The initial idea was to demonstrate how speculative tools could help people develop a vision and basic action plan to navigate climate change in coming decades. I reworked it when COVID-19 hit to think about long-term trajectories for post-pandemic life.

Rather than immediately jumping thirty years into the future, I started by asking people to reflect on what the future might mean for them. How old would attendees be in five years? How old would their parents be? What about their kids, if they had any? What about in ten years? In fifteen? In thirty? What came up for them when they thought about how old they would be in 2050? What might they look like? How would their kids be living?

Only when people felt more grounded in what life in thirty years might mean on personal levels—Would their parents still be alive? Would they?—did we start to look outward, into what surrounding environments could become. Since it was a demonstration workshop, an example of what people could do in their own communities and projects, we focused on information I'd gathered about my home near the San Francisco Bay. We went over projected rates of sea-level rise and flooding on the region's coastal cities, fire rates, air-pollution data, demographic shifts, and potential economic changes. I showed aerial imagery and site photographs to get those who had never been to the area thinking about its forms, topography, and climate. I shared photos of firestorms that had hit in recent years.

We built out ideas of a future world based on that regional context and climatic impact. We asked each other what the Bay might look like in thirty years. What kind of temperatures could hit at midday? What would the air smell like outside? How might kids go to school? If an emergency hit, like a fire, how would the greater city respond? What would happen to traffic? Which areas might be most vulnerable to the flames? What might happen if a firestorm struck at the same time a new pandemic spread?

We broke into groups to discuss and brainstorm more details. I jumped between digital rooms, listening in on people's chats, asking how participants would try to address the impact of the fire individually, the kinds of civic resources they would want available if it was their house that burned down. Where would they want to go? What would a positive outcome

look like? What kinds of systems and plans would allow that positive outcome to occur? What current policies would need to shift? What different
kinds of decisions would be needed to be made now?

We went through the resulting storylines for the better part of an hour.
One group envisioned a future where cities like San Francisco developed
buffer zones around neighborhoods to mitigate the speed and strength of
fire, and give communities more time to escape or dampen the flames. One
of the last groups to share embraced dystopia, depicting the Bay Area as a
place that would do the bare minimum about fire risk and let entire communities burn as long as wealthier centers were safe. People debated the
merits and downfalls of each other's proposals, teasing each other about
being too idealistic or dystopian. They strategized the kind of funding that
could help bury more power lines that so often cause fires to start. They
brainstormed the statewide measures that could support more decentral-
ized energy grids to keep people connected when hazards struck. They
worked with each other to process their fears about the future through
their stories.

A big part of enacting different futures is reshaping the stories we tell ourselves about who we are and where we live. AMP was a way of shifting
the story told about Agbogbloshie, both by outsiders and residents alike.
Rather than a "wasteland," as media stories have called it over the years,[18]
Osseo-Asare and Abbas supported residents to share a different narrative,
one in which Agbogbloshie residents have valuable skills in making, in
repurposing, and in enacting circular economies.

The project created positive impact because it was designed not just
by architects but by the community members themselves. It harnessed
speculative provocation to support people in figuring out the steps needed
to create the futures they wanted to build. Osseo-Asare and Abbas pushed
for this approach by using collaborative speculative design methods that
focused on bigger systemic change. They asked questions like, "What if
goods and services in this area were created and sold in ways that supported

local residents?" and "What if workshop spaces provided better protection to both workers and surrounding environments?" They took the world-building tactic of using provocative questions to create the foundation for Agbogbloshie's future. And they did so while staying rooted in their roles as facilitators and mediators.

Another important feature of the effort is that it was iterative. The concept for the AMP space was developed with members of the AMP Makers Collective over the course of several years. The work, therefore, was as much about process as was about creating a product. It was the outcome of codesigning with more than 1,500 youth and residents from regions as diverse as West Africa, Europe, and the US. Half of the designers were Agbogbloshie residents and grassroots makers; the other half were students and recent grads in STEAM sectors. The result was a

AMP kiosk, AMP (2014).

Testing tools, AMP (2014).

means of amplifying opportunities not just for how spaces are shaped and implemented but also for how the systems used to develop them are redefined.[19]

For a project to be effective, to make lasting change, it cannot simply be made and left. A community's needs change over time. To change with those shifting needs, initiatives have to be embraced by those who live there. It's easier to embrace something that we've helped to make ourselves. It's easier to embrace what we can iterate and refine to adapt to our ideas, desires, and environments as they evolve. When planning mechanisms encourage not just iterative visioning but iterative implementation and adaptation, it's easier to enact desired shifts over time.

Embracing speculative futures in the ways we plan and build our cities can make collaborative iteration the heart of how we develop urban space. When professionals use their skills to facilitate rather than dictate, design becomes a process that celebrates more points of view. It's a context where community members can more effectively advocate for the plans, tools, and projects that suit their actual needs. When residents proactively articulate and shape the futures they want to see, they're better positioned to demand support from planners, designers, and city agencies.

Speculative futures provide tools for people to work through those modes of facilitation, toward the kinds of collaboration that create lasting results. Interacting with future scenarios in tactile, intimate ways allows for stronger long-term thinking, decision-making, and implementation over time.[20] By focusing on the value of facilitation rather than dictation, design and planning can begin to shift toward cocreation, where speculative futures can be enacted to positive effect.[21]

––––––––––––––

The curly haired woman in my Zoom workshop repeated her question: "How do we translate ideas into action?" I was still sipping my water, still delaying my response.

I didn't have a simple answer. I'd been unsuccessful in translating speculative visions of the future into concrete action plenty of times. The future city video game I'd helped to create was designed more to provoke discussion about future change than spark actual planning moves. Earlier projects I had worked on, like the Innovation Center, had failed to translate into built work at all.

The first speculative futures effort I made, the future living room for the art festival in San Francisco, was a provocation-focused exercise as well. It lacked connection to wider planning practices in the city. Festival organizers gave me $2,500 and a few months to put together a world set in 2200. Time and funds were tight. I convinced two remarkable, generous artists[22] to help me create some aspects of the work, but the majority of the research, narrative, and spatial design came down to me.

View seen through false windows of the living room from 2200 (2016).

Exterior view of the living room installation space (2016).

By the time those details were developed, I had little energy or attention left to connect the project to existing planning practices in the city. Doing so had been my original plan. As part of the installation, I'd asked visitors to answer a series of questions before they left: What did the installation make them feel, if anything? What words came to mind when they thought of rising seas? Did they want to see any proactive kinds of changes to prepare in their own neighborhoods?

The questions were designed to learn more about how people related to and talked about climate change. I shared the answers with local city officials once the installation was done, but didn't receive a reply. I hadn't had the bandwidth to coordinate with them beforehand. They might not have been interested in the answers. Because I didn't have the capacity to make coordination a priority, however, I didn't lay the groundwork to effectively find out.

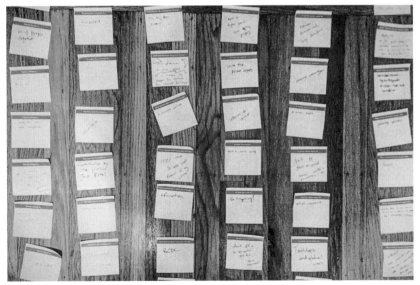

Living room area for sharing responses (top). Selection of responses (bottom) (2016).

If I could do the project over again, I would try harder to link the project to the city's ongoing planning efforts. I would try to make the living room a space where people could connect to and enact their own visions for long-term change. I would try to implement more of the collaborative methods Osseo-Asare and Abbas used in Agbogbloshie, harnessing the story of the living room to invite visitors to rewrite their own narratives about where they lived and worked. I would try to use the installation as a space to build more trust and creativity between planning officials and installation visitors. I would try to raise more funds than what I had been given so I could pay collaborators for their time.

I wanted to tell the woman all of this. I wanted to tell her about the AMP project. I wanted to tell her that when speculative futures are deeply embedded in planning processes, vision can translate into action in ways that don't just have a better chance of sustaining over time, but of adapting to changing conditions. I wanted to acknowledge that there are inherent tensions between what cities want and what communities need, but that it can still be helpful to know what initiatives municipalities are pushing so that creative ideas can complement what's already under way. I wanted to say that it's powerful to do speculative ideation with deadlines for proposals or civic interventions in mind, to create logistical landing pads that can link envisioned futures to present-day projects. Yet the woman was a professional connected to the development world herself. She probably already understood the power of facilitation. She likely knew that there's no single way to link visions into action, that it depends on the work at hand.

There were only a few minutes left in the workshop, so I went for a shorter response: "I don't have the perfect answer for that."

Which is true. There is no perfect way to translate vision into action. Embedding creative speculation in tactical, effective change will always be hard. But it helps when provocative speculation is a valued part of how projects are made. City-making is a balance of political and organizational savvy, imaginative capacity, and technical skill. This is true from architecture and engineering to policy, planning, and construction. In every firm, for a project to get done, someone must know not just how to create safe and effective plans but also how to pull the levers of bureaucracy to move work forward.

To ensure that equity and social resilience play into those dynamics, development has to become more collaborative. Collaboration occurs when city residents don't just participate in planning efforts but coproduce projects as well. This means projects have to take the time, money, and effort to embrace nonprofessional ways of working. It means planning early and proactively. It means establishing long-lasting and respectful relationships, which takes time and patience to cultivate. It means widening the spectrum of worldviews that shape how designs, plans, and development schemes are made.[23] It's hard work.

Speculative futures creates contexts for that hard work to thrive through play, storytelling, and imagination. Using storytelling to center the human narrative can become a powerful tool to cultivate dialogue across differences in expertise, as it did in the future city video game. It can bridge cultural divides, as it did in Columbusplein. It can help connect people and institutions with long-term time scales, as happened in Superflux's UAE project. And it can cultivate deeper degrees of trust, as it did in Agbogbloshie.

Yet speculative futures as an isolated field is not enough. It's not the single answer to the problems our cities face. It's a suite of tools. To be effective, we have to embrace them into the ways we plan and develop. When speculative futures is used to support development that goes beyond inclusion to cocreation, it can be a powerful way to enhance resilience.

If we can stretch our concepts of not just design but also imagination, if we can take the needs, desires, and cares of those beyond ourselves more intimately into account, we might be able to build paths forward from where we are now to more resilient, equitable space. Speculative futures offers approaches that can help. Alone, they won't solve our problems. But if we use them seriously, if we engage in rigorous imaginative play with long-term futures, they can give us the tools to build the cities we need.

CONCLUSION

THE FUTURE IS BORN in the spaces where we allow ourselves to imagine. The events we dream of become the conditions we're more likely to predict. The pictures we develop in our minds are the experiences we most often create. Restricting what we think imagination is for keeps us in the confines of the present day. Valuing the aspirations of certain groups over others creates contexts of mistrust, where many doubt that their needs and opinions will be heard at all. Limiting what we allow ourselves to envision blocks us from weaving the world into a new reality.

We've limited our imaginations of what cities can be for too long. Predictive and persuasive modes of speculation have resulted in urban spaces that perpetuate the status quo. Legacies of inequality, where exclusive development approaches fail to include the concerns of marginalized residents, are metastasizing into crises. By tying our visions of urbanism to doing things the ways they've been done before, we've locked ourselves into conditions primed for dystopian demise.

Speculative futures encourages us to push beyond those limits to create the resilient cities this century demands. Imagining what a future might sound, smell, and taste like provides visceral connections to the impacts of potential change. The more vivid an experience of an alternative future is, the more robust our responses to it become. The stronger our responses become, the deeper our debates about preferred alternatives can go. The more we debate, the more we can identify and enact the futures that work for more of us.

Imagining the future together makes us more resilient. When we feel closer to the impacts of potential change—when the conceptual shifts to the personal—we cultivate greater degrees of concern for our future selves.[1] That concern is fuel. It gives us psychological strength to assess looming danger and explore, articulate, and enact the realities we'd prefer instead. Feeling into what breathing might be like when wildfire seasons are more ferocious allows us to connect to change from a visceral place. Experiencing that visceral connection with others builds the shared language that allows us to collaborate on creating the alternatives we want.[2]

We need the social resilience that imagination fosters more than ever. Technological disruption, ecological extinction, and violent political collapse have already defined the first decades of the twenty-first century, a trend that's only slated to accelerate. COVID-19 was a particularly deadly demonstration of the necessary guidance imagination provides. When the pandemic hit in 2020, shutting down traffic, barricading busy storefronts, and convincing so many people to stay inside that wild animals started taking over town centers, familiarity vanished.[3] What previously felt impossible—global economic shutdown, airborne plague, and grocery-store shelves achingly empty of toilet paper—was happening, and the effects were severe. It was a jarring reminder that old rules can't be relied upon, that the logic of the past isn't enough for what lies ahead.

Navigating modern change depends on imagining futures we've never seen. That tomorrow will be worse than today is far from guaranteed. Where we go from here—whether we accept that dystopian futures are inevitable or start envisioning more resilient spaces—is up to us. To head toward different, potentially better futures, we have to be able to imagine what those futures might be like.[4]

By giving us permission to imagine, speculative futures encourage a shift in attitude from "What's the problem?" to "What's possible?" In doing so, they question our assumptions about existing norms to see if they're really the paradigms we want to shape what lies ahead. Connecting current moves to long-term change helps ensure that the tactics used to solve short-term problems can address the fifty- or one-hundred-year issues as well. Speculative futures offers practices that create the forward-thinking, adaptive plans that modern uncertainty requires.[5]

Perhaps most importantly, the approaches aren't exclusive or special-ized. Using speculative futures doesn't depend on getting a degree or buying expensive software. Anyone can employ them, because everyone has the capacity to imagine. When more people feel empowered to envision their preferred futures, they're more equipped to advocate for their needs. More people promoting the futures they want encourages design and planning professionals to embrace the role of facilitators, to focus less on enacting their own ideas and more on coalescing diverse viewpoints into cohesive plans. In this way, speculative futures cultivates self-determination, creat-ing cities more likely to work not just for the few, but for all.

Embracing speculative futures in how we build requires a revolution in collective mindset. Imagining urban futures has been left to architects, developers, engineers, and planners for long enough. Drawing, modeling, testing, and researching the possibilities of urban space are all part of how professionals learn how to shape cities. Prototyping and iteration is how all projects are made. Yet for most in the development world, the gap between fantasy and reality is less of a space for exploration and play than for pre-diction. People often have their own agendas for how projects should be formed, their own speculative visions to approve and enact. Securing public support is something many see as a box to check off, not a process worth real time and investment.

Speculation can and must do more. For generations, we've built our cities by locking ourselves into end states of imagination. Planners are still trained to push for the masterplan that will fix all problems, even if they don't know whether generated solutions will still be relevant in years to come. Look at the rising numbers of abandoned suburban shopping malls across North America. Once robust centers for civic and commercial life, half of the remaining two thousand are likely to be deserted in the next decade. Or the fields and stadiums left unused in Athens, Greece, once the 2004 Olympic Games ended.[6] Or the city of Brasilia's built-from-scratch design that emphasized cars over people to such a degree that navigating its streets by foot today is near impossible. What seems like a great idea at one time is often revealed as flawed thinking as time goes on. Modern development strives to make things that will last forever, yet rarely accepts that the end state of what is built will always, ultimately, change. Building cities as if the conditions they'll encounter over their lifespans are predictable is not enough for the challenges of these times.

Rather than striving for static perfection, we need cities that work with complexity and change. Predicting the precise timing, scale, and impacts of future transformations, from climate shifts to economic uncertainty to technological acceleration, is impossible. Working with them, however, isn't. When used to provoke new ideas and challenge entrenched modes of thinking, speculative futures can help anticipate big changes and create systems that proactively respond. The approaches translate change from something unknown and scary into a space for imagination, collaboration, and—a word that's too rarely used in city-making—fun. By considering potential visions of what could be, they get us to reflect on the decisions we would rather make today. When you enter a future world, you're participating in a conversation about how life could shift, and how our current realities could be different. Simply placing alternative visions of the future in the public realm provokes deeper, more complex conversation about what we want to create in coming decades.

The tools are a reminder that the future is not a destination, but a process and a path. Speculative futures helps us walk that path—together. By celebrating the space between fantasy and reality, the field invites more people to become active participants in the city-making process. It's a means of asking ourselves deeper questions about the kind of places we want our cities to become. We can use the tools to help each other feel the ramifications of future change, to experience them far enough in advance that effective plans can be developed, iterated, and enacted. We can use our imaginations to increase our agency in building futures in which we can thrive. Doing so beyond the confines of professional design studios ensures that self-determination becomes the foundation for civic life.

By focusing on the value of cooperation rather than dictation, speculative futures reshapes city-making into ground for collaborative action.

Amplifying the diverse perspectives that make up urban life expands our collective imagination of what already exists, and what is possible moving forward. It expands the language we use to talk about what could be. That expanded language increases our collaborative capabilities, enabling more grounded visions of the future to take hold and cultivating the civic support needed for actionable, effective change to occur. When city spaces become more representative of the range of people who call them home, they become more equitable and resilient as a result.

This doesn't mean that expertise has no place in design. Understanding the nuances of structural integrity, the specifics of drought-tolerant plantings, and the energy-efficiency rates of different building materials are just some of the many factors for which trained specialists bring real and necessary value. Understanding how infrastructural systems age, the most effective ways to retrofit existing buildings, and methods for strengthening urban forests as climates shift will be increasingly crucial. Creating contexts where these areas of expertise can respond to the visions and demands of all urban residents holds the key to creating better cities. By helping more of us actively imagine what might be, speculative futures brings that context more immediately to life.

None of this is meant to imply that these tools are a silver bullet. Speculative futures alone is not capable of changing urban development's legacies of inequality and static design. City-making still emphasizes top-down decisions over collaborative planning. Working with people outside professional development teams remains an infrequent move. Personal narratives and local impacts are still too infrequently the focus of the design and planning process. Investigating the human effects of planned changes—the nuance of what living in proposed spaces might be like when someone is sick or has conflicts with a neighbor—is a less-prized piece of the development puzzle.

Whether speculative futures as a field reinforces or reinvents the inequalities embedded in planning systems depends entirely on how its tools are used. Everyone has the power to shape their own narratives. Problems arise when development doesn't allow the diversity of those stories to flourish. Approaches like science fiction prototyping and worldbuilding can just as easily perpetuate racist stereotypes as they can support avenues of mutual empowerment.[7] Conscientiously using them to provoke consideration of different futures can highlight unconscious biases, which helps to challenge the status quo of how cities and systems are made. When used as a means for collaboration rather than persuasion, speculative futures harnesses imagination to create the world in different ways, through more diverse eyes, toward more resilient ends.

This is the time for imagination. If we want to aim toward less-dystopian destinations, we have to get creative. Our survival on this planet depends on cocreating nimble responses to accelerating speeds, scopes, and scales of change. By creating containers for collective imagination of what the future can bring, speculative futures helps us create those responses together.

They do so in part by translating uncertainty into hope. As writer Helen Macdonald recently declared in the *New York Times,* "To keep hope for the future alive we have to consider it as still uncertain, have to believe that concerted, collective human action might yet avert disaster."[8] Speculative futures cultivates that hope by expanding how we articulate what the future can become.

Assuming that devastation is the entirety of what's ahead is limited thinking. What if the best times are still to come? We owe it to ourselves and future generations to ask. The tools to help us ask are there. We just have to use them.

REFERENCES

Abd Elrahman, A. S., and M. Asaad. 2021. "Urban Design and Urban Planning: A Critical Analysis to the Theoretical Relationship Gap." *Ain Shams Engineering Journal* 12, no. 1: 1163–73.

Abdulkarim, K. A. 2017. "Crystallizing a Discourse of 'Khalijiness': Exclusion and Citizenship in the Arab Gulf States." *15 CUREJ: College Undergraduate Research Electronic Journal,* University of Pennsylvania. https://repository .upenn.edu/curej/211.

Adam, B., and C. Groves. 2007. *Future Matters: Action, Knowledge, Ethics.* Leiden, Netherlands: Brill.

Adger, W. N. 2006. "Vulnerability." *Global Environmental Change* 16, no. 3: 268–81.

Adjei, A. 2014. "Life in Sodom and Gomorrah: The World's Largest Digital Dump." *Guardian*, April 29, 2014. https://www.theguardian.com/global -development-professionals-network/2014/apr/29/agbogbloshie-accra-ghana -largest-ewaste-dump.

Adusei, A., J. Arko-Mensah, M. Dzodzomenyo, J. Stephens, A. Amoabeng, S. Waldschmidt, K. Löhndorf et al. 2020. "Spatiality in Health: The Distribution of Health Conditions Associated with Electronic Waste Processing Activities at Agbogbloshie, Accra." *Annals of Global Health* 86, no. 1: 31. http://doi.org /10.5334/aogh.2630.

Albarracín, D. 2021. *Action and Inaction in a Social World: Predicting and Changing Attitudes and Behavior.* Cambridge: Cambridge University Press.

Albrechts, L. 2002. "The Planning Community Reflects on Enhancing Public Involvement: Views from Academics and Reflective Practitioners." *Planning Theory and Research* 3: 331–47.

Aldrich, D., and M. Meyer. 2015. "Social Capital and Community Resilience." *American Behavioral Scientist* 59, no. 2: 254–69. DOI:10.1177/0002764214550299.

Allen, J., G. Cars, and A. Madanipour. 2012. *Social Exclusion in European Cities: Processes, Experiences and Responses.* London: Routledge.

Anti-Eviction Mapping Project. 2021. "Loss of Black Population." http://www
.antievictionmappingproject.net/black.html.

Ammon, R. 2009. "Commemoration amid Criticism: The Mixed Legacy of
Urban Renewal in Southwest Washington, D.C." *Journal of Planning History*
8, no. 3: 175–220.

Anderson, G., and Y. Ge. 2005. "The Size Distribution of Chinese Cities."
Regional Science and Urban Economics 35: 756–76.

Armenakis, A., S. Harris, and H. Field. 1999. "Making Change Permanent: A Model
for Institutionalizing Change Interventions." In *Research in Organizational
Change and Development,* edited by W. Pasmore and R. Woodman, 97–128.
Stamford, CT: JAI Press.

Auger, J. 2013. "Speculative Design: Crafting the Speculation." *Digital Creativity*
24, no. 1: 11–35. https://doi.org/10.1080/14626268.2013.767276.

Austen, I., and D. Wakabayashi. 2020. "Google Sibling Abandons Ambitious
City of the Future in Toronto." *New York Times,* May 7, 2020. https://www
.nytimes.com/2020/05/07/world/americas/google-toronto-sidewalk-labs
-abandoned.html.

Bakare, L. 2014. "Afrofuturism Takes Flight: From Sun Ra to Janelle Monáe."
Guardian, July 24, 2014. https://www.theguardian.com/music/2014/jul/24
/space-is-the-place-flying-lotus-janelle-monae-afrofuturism.

Barber, D. 2013. "Hubbert's Peak, Eneropa, and the Visualization of Renewable
Energy." *Places Journal.* https://placesjournal.org/article/hubberts-peak
-eneropa-and-the-visualization-of-renewable-energy.

Bardzell, J., and S. Bardzell. 2013. "What Is 'Critical' about Critical Design?" In
*CHI 2013: Proceedings of the SIGCHI Conference on Human Factors in Computing
Systems.* 3297–306.

Bartels, K. 2017. "The Double Bind of Social Innovation: Relational Dynamics
of Change and Resistance in Neighbourhood Governance." *Urban Studies* 54,
no. 16: 3789–805.

Bartholomew, K. 2005. "Integrating Land Use Issues into Transportation Planning: Scenario Planning." https://www.semanticscholar.org/paper
/Integrating-Land-Use-Issues-into-Transportation-Bartholomew
/ae56bac9072bf61490bd0e8ccfbfccb847fd2e10.

Bates, L., ed. 2018. "Race and Spatial Imaginary: Planning Otherwise." *Planning
Theory and Practice* 19, no. 2: 254–88. https://doi.org/10.1080/14649357.2018
.1456816.

Batty, M. 2008. "The Size, Scale and Shape of Cities." *Science* 319, no. 5864: 769–71.

Baumann, K. 2017. *Sankofa City.* Video, 6:47. https://vimeo.com/211625350?embedded
=true&source=vimeo_logo&owner=1542672.

———. 2021. Personal communication. June 11, 2021.

Baumann, K., B. Caldwell, F. Bar, and B. Stokes. 2017. "Participatory Design Fiction: Community Storytelling for Speculative Urban Technologies." In *Proceedings of CHI Conference, 2018.* DOI: 10.1145/3170427.3186601.

Beattie, H., D. Brown, and S. Kindon. 2020. "Solidarity through Difference: Speculative Participatory Serious Urban Gaming (SPS-UG)." *International Journal of Architectural Computing* 18, no. 2: 141–54. https://doi.org/10.1177/1478077120924337.

Beauregard, R. 2003. "Democracy, Storytelling, and the Sustainable City." In *Story and Sustainability: Planning, Practice, and Possibility for American Cities,* edited by B. Eckstein and J. Throgmorton, 65–78. Cambridge, MA: MIT Press.

Bennett, E. M. 2003. "Why Global Scenarios Need Ecology." *Frontiers in Ecology and the Environment* 1, no. 6: 322–29.

Bleecker, J. 2009. "Design Fiction: A Short Essay on Design, Science, Fact and Fiction." https://drbfw5wfjlxon.cloudfront.net/writing/DesignFiction_WebEdition.pdf.

Bless, N. 2021. "The Importance of Designing Beyond Inclusion." Hope Idaewor interviews Dr. Dimeji Onafuwa, January 29, 2021, video, 21:34. https://www.youtube.com/watch?v=9GwwkMlsDE4.

Bliss, L. 2018. "How Smart Should a City Be? Toronto Is Finding Out." Bloomberg CityLab. September 7, 2018. https://www.bloomberg.com/news/articles/2018-09-07/what-s-behind-the-backlash-over-sidewalk-labs-smart-city.

———. 2019. "Critics Vow to Block Sidewalk Labs' Controversial Smart City in Toronto." Bloomberg CityLab. February 25, 2019. https://www.bloomberg.com/news/articles/2019-02-25/post-hq2-toronto-residents-try-to-block-sidewalk-labs.

Block, I. 2020. "Masterplanet is Bjark Ingels' plan to redesign Earth and stop climate change." *Dezeen,* October 21, 2020. https://www.dezeen.com/2020/10/27/bjarke-ingels-big-masterplanet-climate-change-architecture-news.

Bloor, S. 2014. "Abandoned Athens Olympic 2004 Venues, 10 Years on—in Pictures." *Guardian,* August 13, 2014. https://www.theguardian.com/sport/gallery/2014/aug/13/abandoned-athens-olympic-2004-venues-10-years-on-in-pictures.

Boal, A. 1992. *Games for Actors and Non-Actors.* 2nd ed. Translated by A. Jackson. London: Routledge.

Bond, S. and M. Thompson-Fawcett. 2006. "Design-Led Participatory Planning." In *Living Together: Towards Inclusive Communities in New Zealand,* edited by M. Thompson-Fawcett and C. Freeman. Dunedin, New Zealand: University of Otago Press.

———. 2007. "Public Participation and New Urbanism: A Conflicting Agenda?" *Planning Theory and Practice* 8, no. 4. DOI: 10.1080/14649350701664689.

Bosker, B. 2018. "We'll Always Have Sky City." *Slate,* January 22, 2018. https:// slate.com/news-and-politics/2018/01/chinas-fake-european-cities-have -been-transformed-into-something-much-more-interesting.html.

Boulding, E. 1988. *Building a Global Civic Culture: Education for an Interdependent World.* Syracuse, NY: Syracuse University Press.

Borchardt, F. 1990. *Doomsday Speculation as a Strategy of Persuasion: A Study of the Apocalypticism as Rhetoric.* Lewiston, NY: Edwin Mellen Press. https://citeseerx .ist.psu.edu/viewdoc/download?doi=10.1.1.40.8471&rep=rep1&type=pdf.

Brahinsky, R. 2019. "Fillmore Revisited: How Redevelopment Tore through the Western Addition." *SF Public Press,* September 23, 2019. https://www .sfpublicpress.org/fillmore-revisited-how-redevelopment-tore-through -the-western-addition.

Bridges, W. 2003. *Managing Transitions: Making the Most of Change.* Cambridge, MA: Perseus.

Brooks, L. A. 2016. "Playing a Minority Forecaster in Search of Afrofuturism: Where Am I in This Future, Stewart Brand?" In *Afrofuturism 2.0: The Rise of Astro-Blackness,* edited by R. Anderson and C. Jones, 149–66. Lanham, MD: Lexington Books.

Brooks, M. P. 1988. "Four Critical Junctures in the History of the Urban Planning Profession: An Exercise in Hindsight." *Journal of the American Planning Association* 54, no. 2: 241–48.

Brown, G. S. 1972. *Laws of Form.* New York: Julian Press.

Burayidi, M. 2000. "Urban Planning as a Multicultural Canon." In *Urban Planning in a Multicultural Society,* edited by M. Burayidi. Westport, CT: Preager.

———. 2003. "The Multicultural City as Planners' Enigma." *Planning Theory and Practice* 4, no. 3: 259–73. https://doi.org/10.1080/1464935032000118634.

Burnam-Fink, M. 2015. "Creating Narrative Scenarios: Science Fiction Prototyping at Emerge." *Futures* 70: 48–55. http://dx.doi.org/10.1016/j.futures .2014.12.005.

Burton, O. 2015. "To Protect and Serve Whiteness." *North American Dialogue* 18, no. 2: 38–50. https://doi.org/10.1111/nad.12032.

Buxton, N. 2017. "Defying Dystopia: Building the Climate Future We Want." *Roar* 7. December 27, 2017. https://roarmag.org/magazine/defying-dystopia-shaping -climate-future-want.

Cabrera, J., and J. Najarian. 2013. "Can New Urbanism Create Diverse Communities?" *Journal of Planning Education and Research.* DOI:10.1177/0739456X13500309.

Cales, R. 2014. "Shenzhen Low Carbon City: A Transformation of Concept and Planning Process." Master's thesis, University of Amsterdam.

Calthorpe, P. 2013. "The Real Problem with China's Ghost Towns." *Metropolis,* September 1, 2013. http://www.metropolismag.com/Point-of-View/August-2013/The-Real-Problem-with-Chinas-Ghost-Towns.

Camara, B. 2006. Appendix F: Geographic Names. In *Pacific Island Network Vital Signs Monitoring Plan,* edited by L. HaySmith, F. L. Klasner, S. H. Stephens, and G. H. Dicus. Natural Resource Report NPS/PACN/NRR—2006/003 National Park Service, Fort Collins, Colorado.

Campanella, T. C. 2011. "Jane Jacobs and the Death and Life of American Planning." In *Reconsidering Jane Jacobs,* edited by M. Page and T. Mennel. Chicago and Washington, DC: American Planning Association.

Candy, S. 2010. *The Futures of Everyday Life: Politics and the Design of Experiential Scenarios.* Honolulu: University of Hawaii at Manoa Press.

———. 2017. "Syrian Refugee Girls Imagine Their Futures." *The Sceptical Futuryst,* June 28, 2017. https:// futuryst.blogspot.com/2017/06/syrian-refugee-girls-imagine-their.html.

———. 2018. "Experiential Futures: A Brief Outline." *The Sceptical Futuryst,* October 31, 2018. https://futuryst.blogspot.com/2018/10/experiential-futures-brief-outline.html

———. 2020. "Introducing Experiential and Participatory Futures at the BBC." *The Sceptical Futuryst,* October 30, 2020. https://futuryst.blogspot.com/2020/10/experiential-futures-at-the-bbc.html.

Candy, S., and J. Dunagan. 2016. "The Experiential Turn." *Human Futures* 1: 26–29.

———. 2017. "Designing an Experiential Scenario: The People Who Vanished." *Futures* 86: 136–53.

Candy, S. and K. Kornet. 2017. "A Field Guide to Ethnographic Experiential Futures." In *Proceedings of Design/Develop/ Transform Conference.* Brussels, Belgium, June 15, 2017. DOI:10.13140/RG.2.2.30623.97448.

———. 2019. "Turning Foresight Inside Out: An Introduction to Ethnographic Experiential Futures." *Journal of Futures Studies* 23, no. 3: 3–22. DOI:10.6531/JFS.201903_23, no. 3.0002.

Carmichael, J. 2016. "How Science Fiction Dystopias Became Blueprints for City Planners." *Inverse,* July 20, 2016. https://www.inverse.com/article/18488-science-fiction-future-city-planning-dubai-skyscrapers-dystopia.

Carpenter, S., B. Walker, J. M. Anderies, and N. Abel. 2001. "From Metaphor to Measurement: Resilience of What to What?" *Ecosystems* 4, no. 8: 765–81.

Carter, J., G. Cavan, A. Connelly, S. Guy, J. Handley, and A. Kazmierczak. 2015. "Climate Change and the City: Building Capacity for Urban Adaptation." *Progress in Planning* 95: 1-66. https://doi.org/10.1016/j.progress.2013.08.001.

Case, T. 2006. "The Commodification and Militarization of American Public Space: From a Genealogy of the Public to a Politics of Place." PhD diss., Florida Atlantic University, Honors College.

Chakraborty, A., and A. McMillan. 2015. "Scenario Planning for Urban Planners: Toward a Practitioner's Guide." *Journal of the American Planning Association* 81: 1. DOI:10.1080/01944363.2015.1038576.

Chakraborty, A., N. Kaza, G. J. Knaap and B. Deal. 2011. "Robust Plans and Contingent Plans." *Journal of the American Planning Association,* 77, no. 3: 251–66. DOI:lo.1080/01944363.2011.582394.

Chang, C. 2010. "I Wish This Was." http://candychang.com/work/i-wish-this-was.

Chermack, T. J., and L. M. Coons. 2015. "Integrating Scenario Planning and Design Thinking: Learnings from the 2014 Oxford Futures Forum." *Futures* 74: 71–77.

Chu, H., and J. Yang. 2019. "Emotion and the Psychological Distance of Climate Change." *Science Communication* 41, no. 6: 761–89. https://journals.sagepub.com/doi/10.1177/1075547019889637.

Chu, H., and J. Yang. 2018. "Taking Climate Change Here and Now: Mitigating Ideological Polarization with Psychological Distance." *Global Environmental Change* 53: 174–81. https://www.sciencedirect.com/science/article/abs/pii/S0959378018301249.

City of Oakland. 2020. "Oakland Slow Streets General Feedback Survey Results." https://www.oaklandca.gov/resources/slow-street-corridor-evaluation-and-essential-places-improvements.

———. 2021. "Oakland Slow Streets." https://www.oaklandca.gov/projects/oakland-slow-streets.

Cocchia, A. 2014. "Smart and Digital City: A Systematic Literature Review." In *Smart City: How to Create Public and Economic Value with High Technology in Urban Space,* edited by R. P. Dameri and C. Rosenthal-Sabroux, 13–44. Cham, Switzerland: Springer.

Collie, B. 2011. "Cities of the Imagination: Science Fiction, Urban Space, and Community Engagement in Urban Planning." *Futures* 43, no. 4: 424–31.

Corbin, C. N. E. 2018. "(Re)Imagining Racialized Urban Environmentally Just Futures . . ." In "Race and Spatial Imaginary: Planning Otherwise," edited by L. Bates. *Planning Theory and Practice* 19, no. 2: 254–88. DOI:10.1080/14649357.2018.1456816.

Coulton, P., D. Burnett, and A. Gradinar. 2016. "Games as Speculative Design: Allowing Players to Consider Alternate Presents and Plausible Futures." Paper presented at the 2016 Design Research Society 50th Anniversary Conference, Brighton, UK June 20–27, 2016. https://pdfs.semanticscholar.org/700b /2cfae4491b50dafc7d51cb98c875688b619.pdf?_ga=2.129423241.485269973 .1618937646-456665089.1618937646.

Crowe, B., J. S. Gaulton, N. Minor, D. A. Asch, J. Eyet, E. Rainosek, K. Flint et al. 2022. "To Improve Quality, Leverage Design." *BMJ Quality and Safety* 31: 70–74. DOI:10.1136/bmjqs-2021-013605.

Crowe, C. 2021. "Waterfront Toronto to Design 'Complete Community' after Sidewalk Labs Split." *Smart Cities Dive,* March 17, 2021. https://www .smartcitiesdive.com/news/waterfront-toronto-to-design-complete-community -after-sidewalk-labs-split/596748.

Dassé, M. 2019. "The Neoliberalization of Public Spaces and the Infringement of Civil Liberties: The Case of the Safer Cities Initiative in Los Angeles." *Angles. New Perspectives on the Anglophone World* 8.

Data USA. 2001. https://datausa.io.

Dator, J. 2005. Foreword in *The Knowledge Base of Futures Studies,* edited by R. Slaughter. Indooroopilly, Australia: Foresight International.

———. 2019. "Futures Studies as Applied Knowledge." In *Jim Dator: A Noticer in Time, Selected Work, 1967–2018.* New York: Springer.

Davis, M. 2006. *City of Quartz: Excavating the Future in Los Angeles.* Brooklyn, NY: Verso Books.

Day, W. R., and Supreme Court of the United States. 1917. U.S. Reports: Buchanan v. Warley, 245 U.S. 60.

de Graaf, R. 2010. "TEDxRotterdam – Reinier de Graff – Roadmap to zero carbon Europe." TED video, 13:15. November 10, 2019. https://www.youtube.com /watch?v=VCRSk1itoRU.

de Monchaux, N. 2020. "The Spaces That Make Cities Fairer and More Resilient." *New York Times.* May 12, 2020. https://www.nytimes.com/2020/05/12/opinion /sunday/cities-public-space-covid.html.

Deck, K. 2019. "Enviro-Envision: Visualizing Climate Change through Art." Master's thesis. University of California, Santa Cruz. https://escholarship.org /content/qt1nn1f5kn/qt1nn1f5kn_noSplash_9afacf089892f892613486509964403a .pdf?t=puqde4.

Design nl. 2014. "The People's Democratic Republic of Columbusplein." June 2, 2014. http://www.design.nl/item/the_peoples_democratic_republic_of _columbusplein.

Desowitz, B. 2018. "The Unique Challenge of World Building in 'Black Panther,' 'First Man,' and 'The Favourite.'" IndieWire. November 15, 2018. https:// www.indiewire.com/2018/11/black-panther-first-man-the-favourite-world -building-production-design-1202020977.

Directory of African American Architects. 2021. https://blackarchitect.us.

Dobraszczyk, P. 2019. *Future Cities: Architecture and the Imagination*. London: Reaktion books.

Doctoroff, D. 2016. "Reimagining Cities from the Internet Up." Medium. https:// medium.com/sidewalk-talk/reimagining-cities-from-the-internet-up -5923d6be63ba.

Dörrer, K. 2016. "What Has Become of China's Ghost Cities?" DW. November 25, 2016. https://www.dw.com/en/what-has-become-of-chinas-ghost-cities/a -36525007.

Dubai Electricity and Water Authority. "DEWA the Brand." https://www.dewa .gov.ae/en/about-dewa/about-us/about-us/dewa-the-brand.

Dulic, A., J. Angel, and S. Sheppard. 2016. "Designing Futures: Inquiry in Climate Change Communication." *Futures* 81: 54–67.

Dunagan, J., and S. Candy. 2007. *Foundfutures: Chinatown—Community Futures Initiative*. Report submitted to the Hawaii Arts Alliance. https://www.scribd .com/doc/298048071/Dunagan-and-Candy-2007-FoundFutures-Chinatown.

Dunne, A., and F. Raby. 2007. "Critical Design FAQ." Dunne and Raby. http:// www.dunneandraby.co.uk/content/bydandr/13/0.

———. 2013. *Speculative Everything: Design, Fiction, and Social Dreaming*. Cambridge, MA: MIT Press.

Durfee, T., and M. Zeiger, eds. 2017. *Made Up: Design's Fictions*. New York: Art-Center Graduate Press / Actar.

Duyar, Y. E., and A. Andreotti. 2015. "Interview: Liam Young on Speculative Architecture And Engineering The Future." *Next Nature*. March 29, 2015. https://nextnature.net/story/2015/interview-liam-young.

Eagly, A. H., and S. Sczesny. 2019. "Gender Roles in the Future? Theoretical Foundations and Future Research Directions." *Frontiers in Psychology* 10. DOI=10.3389/fpsyg.2019.01965.

Earl, A., and D. Albarracín. 2007. "Nature, Decay, and Spiraling of the Effects of Fear-Inducing Arguments and HIV Counseling and Testing: A Meta-Analysis of the Short- and Long-Term Outcomes of HIV-Prevention Interventions." *Health Psychology* 26, no. 4: 496-506. https://docs.wixstatic.com /ugd/e3eff4_7e50a2b489ed4443901cd7154d4c7dc8.pdf.

Eckersley, R. 1997. "Portraits of Youth: Understanding Young People's Relationship with the Future." *Futures* 29, no. 3: 243–49.

Elliott-Cooper, A., R. Hubbard, and L. Lees. 2019. "Moving beyond Marcuse: Gentrification, Displacement and the Violence of Un-Homing." *Progress in Human Geography* 44, no. 3: 492–509. https://doi.org/10.1177/0309132519830511.

Enfors, E., L. Gordon, G. Peterson, and D. Bossio. 2008. "Making Investments in Dryland Development Work: Participatory Scenario Planning in the Makanya Catchment, Tanzania." *Ecology and Society* 13, no. 4.

Eng, K. 2014. "How to Build a Micronation: Fellows Friday with Artist Jorge Mañes Rubio." TED. January 24, 2014. https://blog.ted.com/how-to-build -a-micronation.

Escobar, A. 2018. *Designs for the Pluriverse: Radical Interdependence, Autonomy, and the Making of Worlds.* Durham, NC: Duke University Press.

Evans, L. S., C. C. Hicks, P. Fidelman, R. C. Tobin, and A. L. Perry. 2013. "Future Scenarios as a Research Tool: Investigating Climate Change Impacts, Adaptation Options and Outcomes for the Great Barrier Reef, Australia." *Human Ecology: An Interdisciplinary Journal* 41: 841–57.

Fermoso, J. 2020. "What Do We Know about Slow Streets and Safety? Here's What Data and Residents Have to Say." *The Oaklandside.* November 25, 2020. https://oaklandside.org/2020/11/25/what-do-we-know-about-slow-streets-and -safety-heres-what-data-and-residents-have-to-say.

Ferri, G., J. Bardzell, S. Bardzell, and S. Louraine. 2014. "Analyzing Critical Designs: Categories, Distinctions, and Canons of Exemplars." In *Proceedings of DIS Conference.* ACM Press: 355–64.

Fisher, M. 2009. *Capitalist Realism: Is There No Alternative?* Winchester, UK: John Hunt.

Flatow, N. 2018. "The Social Responsibility of Wakanda's Golden City." Bloomberg CityLab. November 5, 2018. https://www.bloomberg.com/news /articles/2018-11-05/how-hannah-beachler-built-black-panther-s-wakanda.

Foerster, H. 1973. "On Constructing a Reality." http://pespmc1.vub.ac.be/books /Foerster-constructingreality.pdf.

Forester, J. 1989. *Planning in the Face of Power.* Los Angeles: University of California Press.

———. 1999. *The Deliberative Practitioner: Encouraging Participatory Planning Processes.* London: MIT Press.

Frayling, C. 1993. "Research in Art and Design." *Royal College of Art Research Papers,* 1, no. 1: 1–5.

Freemark, Y. (@yfreemark). 2018. "I don't really understand how the trains work in terms of where they stop, etc, but the pedestrian streets and building density in Wakanda are fantastic!" Twitter, February 18, 2018, 8:40 p.m. https://twitter.com/yfreemark/status/965400664581996544?ref_src

=twsrc%5Etfw%7Ctwcamp%5Etweetembed%7Ctwterm%5E9654006645819
96544%7Ctwgr%5E%7Ctwcon%5Es1_&ref_url=https%3A%2F%2Farchive
.curbed.com%2F2018%2F2%2F19%2F17028794%2Fblack-panther-wakanda
-urban-design-architecture-birnin-zana.

Freestone, R, ed. 2000. *Urban Planning in a Changing World: The Twentieth Century Experience.* London: Routledge.

Folke, C., S. R. Carpenter, B. Walker, M. Scheffer, T. Chapin, and J. Rockström. 2010. "Resilience Thinking: Integrating Resilience, Adaptability and Transformability." *Ecology and Society* 15, no. 4: 20.

Foth, M., B. Bajracharya, R. Brown, and G. Hearn. 2009. "The Second Life of Urban Planning? Using NeoGeography Tools for Community Engagement." *Journal of Location Based Services* 3, no. 2: 91–117.

Fu, Y., and X. Zhang. 2017. "Planning for Sustainable Cities? A Comparative Content Analysis of the Master Plans of Eco, Low-Carbon and Conventional New Towns in China." *Habitat International* 63: 55–66. https://doi.org/10.1016/j.habitatint.2017.03.008.

———. 2018. "Two Faces of an Eco-City? Sustainability Transition and Territorial Rescaling of a New Town in Zhuhai." *Land Use Policy* 18: 627–36. https://doi.org/10.1016/j.landusepol.2018.06.007.

Fuchs, S., and T. Thaler. 2018. *Vulnerability and Resilience to Natural Hazards.* New York: Cambridge University Press.

Fullilove, M. T. 2004. *Root Shock.* New York: Random House.

Fussell, S. 2018. "The City of the Future Is a Data-Collection Machine." *The Atlantic.* https://www.theatlantic.com/technology/archive/2018/11/google-sidewalk-labs/575551.

Gaesser, B. 2013. "Constructing Memory, Imagination, and Empathy: A Cognitive Neuroscience Perspective." *Frontiers in Psychology* 3, 576.

Ganis, M. 2015. *Planning Urban Places: Self-Organising Places with People in Mind.* New York: Routledge.

Gans, H. J. 1966. "The Failure of Urban Renewal." In *Urban Renewal: The Record and the Controversy,* edited by James Q. Wilson. Cambridge, MA: MIT Press.

Gaver, W. 2012. "What Should We Expect from Research through Design?" In *Proceedings of CHI 2012,* 937–46.

Gidley, J. M. 2017. *The Future: A Very Short Introduction.* Oxford: Oxford University Press.

Gebru, T. 2020. "Data-Driven Claims about Race and Gender Perpetuate the Negative Biases of the Day." In *The Oxford Handbook of Ethics of AI,* edited by D. Dubber, F. Pasquale, S. Das. Oxford: Oxford University Press.

Gioia, T. (@tedgioia). 2020. "Can you guess which of these is concept art for Blade Runner 2049 and which is the current San Francisco skyline?" Twitter, September 10, 2020, 4:17 p.m. https://twitter.com/tedgioia/status /1304151979992776705?lang=en.

Ghamari-Tabrizi, S. 2009. *The Worlds of Herman Kahn*. Cambridge, MA: Harvard University Press.

Goetz, E., R. A. Williams, and A. Damiano. 2020. "Whiteness and Urban Planning." *Journal of the American Planning Association* 86, no. 2: 142–56. DOI:10.1080 /01944363.2019.1693907.

Gold J. R. 2001. "Under Darkened Skies: The City in Science-Fiction Film." *Geography* 86, no. 4: 337–45. http://www.jstor.org/stable/40573613.

Goldstein, B. and W. H. Butler. 2010. "The US Fire Learning Network: Providing a Narrative Framework for Restoring Ecosystems, Professions, Institutions." *Society and Natural Resources*, 23, no. 10: 1–17.

Goldstein, B., A. Wessells, R. Lejano and W. Butler. 2013. "Narrating Resilience: Transforming Urban Systems through Collaborative Storytelling." *Urban Studies* 52, no. 7: 1285–303.

Golubiewski, N. 2012. "Is There a Metabolism of an Urban Ecosystem? An Ecological Critique." *AMBIO* 41: 751–64. https://doi.org/10.1007/s13280-011-0232-7.

Goodspeed, R. 2017. "An Evaluation Framework for the Use of Scenarios in Urban Planning." Lincoln Institute of Land Policy, University of Michigan. https://www.lincolninst.edu/sites/default/files/pubfiles/goodspeed_wp17rgi.pdf.

Governa, F., and A. Sampieri. 2019. "Urbanisation Processes and New Towns in Contemporary China: A Critical Understanding from a Decentred View." *Urban Studies* 57, no. 2: 366–82.

Graham, G., A. Greenhill, and V. Callaghan. 2014. "Technological Forecasting and Social Change Special Section: Creative Prototyping." *Technological Forecasting and Social Change* 84: 1–4.

Green, B. 2019a. "The Smart Enough City: Lessons from the Past and a Framework for the Future." MIT Press Blog. https://smartenoughcity.mitpress.mit .edu/pub/olgoe4s8/release/1.

———. 2019b. *The Smart Enough City*. Boston: MIT Press.

———. 2019c. "Cities Are Not Technology Problems: What Smart Cities Companies Gets Wrong." *Metropolis*. https://www.metropolismag.com/cities /ben-green-smart-enough-city.

Haggart, B., and B. Tusikov. 2020. "Sidewalk Labs' Smart-City Plans for Toronto Are Dead. What's Next?" The Conversation. https://theconversation.com /sidewalk-labs-smart-city-plans-for-toronto-are-dead-whats-next-138175.

Hales, D. 2013. "Design Fictions: An Introduction and Provisional Taxonomy." *Digital Creativity* 24, no. 1: 1–10.

Hall, P., and C. Ward. 2000. "Sociable Cities: The Legacy of Ebenezer Howard." *Architectural Research Quarterly* 4: 91.

Hanna J. and S. Ashby. 2016. "From Design Fiction to Future Models of Community Building and Civic Engagement." In *Proceedings of the 9th Nordic Conference on Human-Computer Interaction*, ACM Press.

Hansen, S. 2020. "Feelings of (Un)safety in the Netherlands." Master's thesis, Radboud University Nijmegen. https://theses.ubn.ru.nl/bitstream/handle /123456789/9167/Hansen%2C_Senna_1.pdf?sequence=1.

Hardesty, L. 2013. "Why Innovation Thrives in Cities." MIT News Office. June 4, 2013. https://news.mit.edu/2013/why-innovation-thrives-in-cities-0604.

Haridy, R. 2018. "Science Fiction Cities: How Our Future Visions Influence the Cities We Build." *New Atlas,* July 28, 2018. https://newatlas.com/science -fiction-cities-future-urban-visions-architecture/55569.

Hartman, C. 1964. "The Housing of Relocated Families." *Journal of the American Institute of Planners* (November).

———. 1984. *The Transformation of San Francisco.* Totowa, NJ: Rowman and Allanheld.

Hartman, H. 2010. "Rotterdam, the Netherlands—Rem Koolhass' OMA Tackles Energy Interdependency in Europe." *Architectural Review.* https://www .architectural-review.com/essays/rotterdam-the-netherlands-rem-koolhaas -oma-tackles-energy-interdependency-in-europe.

Harvard University. 2022. "The Department of Urban Planning and Design." https://www.gsd.harvard.edu/urban-planning-design.

Hawkins, A. 2019. "Alphabet's Sidewalk Labs Unveils Its High-Tech 'City-within-a-City' Plan for Toronto." The Verge. https://www.theverge .com/2019/6/24/18715486/alphabet-sidewalk-labs-toronto-high-tech -city-within-a-city-plan.

Healey P. 1997. *Collaborative Planning: Shaping Places in Fragmented Societies.* London: MacMillan Press Ltd.

Heeyoung, J. 2019. "Planning New Cities as New Economic Engines in China." MCP Thesis, MIT, Department of Urban Studies and Planning.

Henry, B. 2015. "The Educator at the Crossroads of Institutional Change." *Journal of Museum Education* 3, no. 31: 223–32.

Hernandez, J. 2009. "Redlining Revisited: Mortgage Lending Patterns in Sacramento 1930–2004." *International Journal of Urban and Regional Research* 33, no. 2: 291–313.

Hicks, D. 2002. *Lessons for the Future: The Missing Dimension in Education.* London: Routledge Falmer.

Hobson, J. 1999. *New Towns, the Modernist Planning Project and Social Justice: The Cases of Milton Keynes, UK, and 6th October Egypt.* London: University College London.

Hoch, C. 1994. *What Planners Do.* Chicago: Planners Press.

Holler, CQ 2017. "The Experiential Futures of Futureproof: A Format for Improvising Future Scenarios." MDes Project. Faculty of Design, OCAD University. http://openresearch.ocadu.ca/id/eprint/1987.

Holt, J. 2011. "Two Brains Running." *New York Times,* November 27, 2011, https://www.nytimes.com/2011/11/27/books/review/thinking-fast-and-slow-by-daniel-kahneman-book-review.html.

Höök, K., P. Dalsgaard, S. Reeves, J. Bardzell, J. Löwgren, E. Stolterman, and Y. Rogers. 2015. "Knowledge Production in Interaction Design." In *Proceedings of the 33rd Annual ACM Conference Extended Abstracts on Human Factors in Computing Systems:* 2429–32.

Höök, K., and J. Löwgren. 2012. "Strong Concepts: Intermediate-Level Knowledge in Interaction Design Research." *ACM Transactions on Computer-Human Interaction* 19, no. 3: 1–18.

Hopkins, L. D., and M. Zapata, eds. 2007. *Engaging the Future: Forecasts, Scenarios, Plans, and Projects.* Cambridge, MA: Lincoln Institute of Land Policy.

Horelli, L. 2007. "A Methodological Approach to Children's Participation in Urban Planning." *Scandinavian Housing and Planning Research* 14, no. 3: 105–15.

Hurley, K. 2008. "Is That a Future We Want? An Ecofeminist Exploration of Images of the Future in Contemporary Film." *Futures* 40: 346–59.

Hutchinson, F. P. 1996. *Educating Beyond Violent Futures.* London: Routledge.

Hyphen-Labs. 2017. "NeuroSpeculative AfroFeminism." http://www.hyphen-labs.com/nsaf.html.

Imarisha, W., and A. Brown, eds. 2015. *Octavia's Brood: Science Fiction Stories from Social Justice Movements.* Oakland, CA: AK Press.

Inayatullah, S. 1998. "Causal Layered Analysis: Poststructuralism as Method." *Futures* 30, no. 8: 815–29.

Innes, J. 1996. "Planning Theory's Emerging Paradigm: Communicative Action and Interactive Practice." *Journal of Planning Education and Research* 14: 128–35.

Inspirock. 2020. "Xingyuan Lake Park, Hanzhong." https://www.inspirock.com/china/hanzhong/xingyuan-lake-park-a469910159.

IPCC. 2012. "Special Report: Managing the Risks of Extreme Events and Disasters to Advance Climate Change Adaptation (SREX)." Cambridge.

Irving, A. 1993. "The Modern/Postmodern Divide in Urban Planning." *University of Toronto Quarterly* (Summer): 474–88.

Isserman, A. 1985. "Dare to Plan: An Essay on the Role of the Future in Planning Practice and Education." *Town Planning Review* 56, no. 4: 483–91.

Jackson, E. 2019. "Biidaaban: First Light." MFA thesis, York University, Toronto, Ontario. https://core.ac.uk/download/pdf/223242153.pdf.

Jacobs, H. 2018. "I Stayed at a Hotel on Dubai's Massive Artificial Island Shaped Like a Palm Tree and It's More Surreal Than Any Photos Can Show." *Insider,* December 3, 2018. https://www.businessinsider.com/dubai-palm-jumeirah -artificial-island-2018-12.

Jacobs, J. 1961. *The Death and Life of Great American Cities.* New York: Random House.

Jain, A. 2017. "Why We Need to Imagine Different Futures." TED video, 14:32. https://www.ted.com/talks/anab_jain_why_we_need_to_imagine_different _futures/transcript?langu.

Jiang, Y., H. Luyao, T. Shi, and Q. Gui. "A Review of Urban Planning Research for Climate Change." *Sustainability* 9, no. 12: 2224.

Johnson, B. D. 2009. "Science Fiction Prototypes Or: How I Learned to Stop Worrying about the Future and Love Science Fiction." In *Intelligent Environments 2009, Proceedings of the 5th International Conference on Intelligent Environments,* edited by V. Callaghan and A. Kameas. Amsterdam: IOS Press BV.

———. 2011. *Science Fiction Prototyping: Designing the Future with Science Fiction.* San Rafael, CA: Morgan and Claypool.

Johnson, I. 2013. "China's Great Uprooting: Moving 250 Million Into Cities." *New York Times,* June 15, 2013. http://www.nytimes.com/2013/06/16/world/asia /chinas-great-uprooting-moving-250-million-into-cities.html?pagewanted =all&_r=0.

Johnson, K. A., G. Dana, N. Jordan, K. Draeger, A. Kapuscinski, L. Schmitt Olabisi, and P. Reich. 2012. "Using Participatory Scenarios to Stimulate Social Learning for Collaborative Sustainable Development." *Ecology and Society* 17, no. 2.

Johnstone, K. 1981. *Impro: Improvisation and the Theatre.* London: Methuen.

Jordan, F. 2016. "San Francisco Continues Destruction of Its Black Community." *San Francisco Chronicle,* April 28, 2016. https://www.sfchronicle.com /opinion/openforum/article/San-Francisco-continues-destruction-of-its -black-7382364.php.

Kaboli, S. A., and Tapio, P. 2018. "How Late-Modern Nomads Imagine Tomorrow? A Causal Layered Analysis Practice to Explore the Images of the Future of Young Adults." *Futures* 96: 32–43.

Kahn, H. 1962. *Thinking about the Unthinkable*. New York: Horizon Press.

Kahneman, D. 2011. *Thinking, Fast and Slow*. New York: Farrar Straus and Giroux.

Kaufman, S. 2011. "Complex Systems, Anticipation, and Collaborative Planning for Resilience." In *Collaborative Resilience: Moving through Crisis to Opportunity*, edited by B. E. Goldstein, 61–98. Cambridge, MA: MIT Press.

Keck, M., and P. Sakdapolrak. 2013. "What Is Social Resilience? Lessons Learned and Ways Forward." *Erdkunde: Archive for Scientific Geography* 67, no. 1: 5–19.

Keen, S. 2006. "A Theory of Narrative Empathy." *Narrative* 14, no. 3: 207–36.

Kelliher, A., and D. Byrne. 2015. "Design Futures in Action: Documenting Experiential Futures for Participatory Audiences." *Futures* 70: 36–47.

Kelly, K. (@kevin2kelly). 2014. "I don't believe in utopia. I believe in protopia — that through progress and process tomorrow will be slightly better than today." Twitter, April 18, 2014, 2:00 p.m. https://twitter.com/kevin2kelly/status/457217022716166144?lang=en.

Khubaev A. O., S. S. Saakyan, and N. V. Makaev. 2020. "World Practice in the Field of Modular Construction." *Construction and Geotechnics* 11, no. 2: 99–108. DOI:10.15593/2224-9826/2020.2.09.

Kimmelman, M. 2021. "How Can Blackness Construct America?" *New York Times,* March 11, 2021. https://www.nytimes.com/2021/03/11/arts/design/black-architecture-moma.html.

Kimmerer, R. W. 2013. *Braiding Sweetgrass*. Minneapolis, MN: Milkweed.

Kirtley, D. "Dystopian Fiction's Popularity Is a Warning Sign for the Future." *Wired,* December 20, 2014. https://www.wired.com/2014/12/geeks-guide-naomi-klein.

Kitchin, R. 2014. "The Real-Time City? Big Data and Smart Urbanism." *GeoJournal* 79, 1–14.

Klein, J. 2008. "A Community Lost: Urban Renewal and Displacement in San Francisco's Western Addition District." UC Berkeley. Master's thesis, University of California, Berkeley. https://citeseerx.ist.psu.edu/viewdoc/download?doi=10.1.1.598.194&rep=rep1&type=pdf.

Klinenberg, E. 2013. "Adaptation: How Can Cities Be 'Climate-Proofed'?" *New Yorker,* January 7, 2013. http://www.newyorker.com/reporting/2013/01/07/130107fa_fact_klinenberg.

Klosterman, R. E. 2014. "Lessons Learned about Planning." *Journal of the American Planning Association* 79, no. 2: 161–69.

Kolb, D. 2015. Experiential Learning: Experience as the Source of Learning and Development. 2nd ed. Upper Saddle River, NJ: Pearson Education.

Kornet, K. 2015. "Causing an Effect: Activists, Uncertainty and Images of the Future." Master in Design Studies Project. OCAD University, Faculty of Design.

Kunstler, J. 2008. World Made by Hand. New York: Atlantic Monthly Press.

Krumholz, N. 1996, 2003. "Equitable Approaches to Local Economic Development." In Readings in Planning Theory, 2nd ed., edited by S. Campbell and S. S. Fainstein, 224–36. Oxford: Blackwell.

Kulhan, B., and C. Crisafulli. 2017. Getting to "Yes And": The Art of Business Improv. Stanford, CA: Stanford University Press.

Kuzmanovic, M., and N. Gaffney. 2017. "Enacting Futures in Postnormal Times." Future 86: 107–17.

Krznaric, R. 2020. The Good Ancestor: A Radical Prescription for Long-Term Thinking. New York: The Experiment.

LA2050. 2016. "Sankofa City." https://archive.la2050.org/2016/sankofa-city.

Lane, H., R. Morello-Frosch, J. Marshall, and J. Apte. 2022. "Historical Redlining Is Associated with Present-Day Air Pollution Disparities in U.S. Cities." Environmental Science and Technology Letters. doi 10.1021/acs.estlett.1c01012.

Larsen, H., and A. Hansen. 2008. "Gentrification—Gentle or Traumatic? Urban Renewal Policies and Socioeconomic Transformations in Copenhagen." Urban Studies 45, no. 12: 2429–48. https://doi.org/10.1177/0042098008097101.

Le Corbusier, C. 1929. The City of Tomorrow and Its Planning. London: John Rodher Press.

———. 1971. Looking at City Planning. New York: Grossman.

Ledogar, R. J., and J. Fleming. 2008. "Social Capital and Resilience: A Review of Concepts and Selected Literature Relevant to Aboriginal Youth Resilience Research." Pimatisiwin 6, no. 2: 25–46.

Lee, K. (@Klee_FilmReview). 2020. "It is LITERALLY Blade Runner 2049 in California right now." Twitter, September 9, 2020, 1:34 p.m. https://twitter.com/Hamza_Maaster/status/1304210770926931970.

Lees, L. 2000. "A Reappraisal of Gentrification: Towards a 'Geography of Gentrification.'" Progress in Human Geography 24, no. 3: 389–408.

Legacy, C. 2017. "Is There a Crisis in Participatory Planning?" Planning Theory 16, no. 4: 425–42.

Lejano, R., and R. Wessells. 2013. "Community and Economic Development: Seeking Ground in Discourse and in Practice." Urban Studies 43, no. 9: 1469–89.

Lepore, J. 2017. "A Golden Age for Dystopian Fiction." *New Yorker,* June 5, 2017. https://www.newyorker.com/magazine/2017/06/05/a-golden-age-for -dystopian-fiction.

Levin, S. 2019. " 'There's No Way to Stop This': Oakland Braces for the Arrival of Tech Firm Square." *Guardian,* July 2, 2019. https://www.theguardian.com /cities/2019/jul/02/theres-no-way-to-stop-this-oakland-braces-for-the-arrival -of-tech-firm-square.

Li, L., Z. Xiao, S. Luo, and A. Yang. 2020. "Projected Changes in Precipitation Extremes over Shaanxi Province, China, in the 21st Century." *Advances in Meteorology* 20. https://doi.org/10.1155/2020/1808404.

Linán, F., and A. Fayolle. 2015. "A Systematic Literature Review on Entrepreneurial Intentions: Citation, Thematic Analyses, and Research Agenda." *International Entrepreneurship and Management Journal* 11, no. 4: 907–33.

Lindley, J. 2015. "Researching Design Fiction with Design Fiction." In *Proceedings of the 2015 ACM SIGCHI Conference on Creativity and Cognition,* June, 2015. 325–26.

List, D. 2004. "Multiple Pasts, Converging Presents, and Alternative Futures." *Futures* 36: 23–43.

Ljubenovic, M., P. Mitkovic, and M. Mitkovic. 2013. "The Scenario Method in Urban Planning." *Architecture and Civil Engineering* 12, no. 1: 81–95.

Longstreth, R. 2006. "The Difficult Legacy of Urban Renewal." *Journal of Heritage Stewardship* 3, no. 1: 6–23.

Lowe, T., K. Brown, S. Dessal, M. De, M. F. Doria, K. Haynes, and K. Vincent. 2006. "Does Tomorrow Ever Come? Disaster Narrative and Public Perceptions of Climate Change." *Public Understanding of Science* 15: 435–57. https://www.climateprediction.net/wp-content/schools/tyndall _DAT.pdf.

Lowndes, V., L. Pratchett, and G. Stoker. 2001. "Trends in Public Participation: Part 1—Local Government Perspectives." *Public Administration* 79, no. 1: 205–22.

———. 2001. "Trends in Public Participation: Part 2—Citizen's Perspectives." *Public Administration* 79, no. 2: 445–55.

Lund, H. 2002. "Pedestrian Environments and Sense of Community." *Journal of Planning Education and Research* 2, no. 3: 301–12. DOI:10.1177/0739456X020210 0307.

———. 2003. "Testing the Claims of New Urbanism: Local Access, Pedestrian Travel, and Neighboring Behaviors." *Journal of the American Planning Association* 51, no. 4. DOI:0.1080/01944360308976328.

Lynch, K. 1960. *The Image of the City.* Cambridge, MA: MIT Press

———. 1965. "An Analysis of the Visual Form of Brookline, Massachusetts." In *City Sense and City Design: Writings and Projects of Kevin Lynch,* edited by T. Banerjee and M. Southworth, 287–315. Cambridge, MA: MIT Press.

———. 1985. "Reconsidering the Image of the City." In *City Sense and City Design: Writings and Projects of Kevin Lynch,* edited by T. Banerjee and M. Southworth, 247–56. Cambridge, MA: MIT Press.

———. 1990. "The Visual Shape of the Shapeless Metropolis." In *City Sense and City Design: Writings and Projects of Kevin Lynch,* edited by T. Banerjee and M. Southworth, 65–86. Cambridge, MA: MIT Press.

Macdonald, H. 2020. *Vesper Flights.* Grove Press.

———. 2021. "The Man Who Finally Made a 'Dune' That Fans Will Love: How Denis Villeneuve Broke the Curse." *New York Times,* October 13, 2021. https://www.nytimes.com/2021/10/13/magazine/dune-denis-villeneuve.html.

Maclean, K., M. Cuthill, and H. Ross. 2014. "Six Attributes of Social Resilience." *Journal of Environmental Planning and Management* 57, no. 1.

Madanipour, A. 2015. "Social Exclusion and Space." In *The City Reader,* 6th ed., edited by R. LeGates and F. Stout, 237–45. London: Routledge.

Mager, C., and L. Matthey. 2015. "Tales of the City: Storytelling as a Contemporary Tool of Urban Planning and Design." *Journal of Urban Research* 7. https://journals.openedition.org/articulo/2779.

Malinga, R., L. Gordon, R. Lindborg, and G. Jewitt. 2013. "Using Participatory Scenario Planning to Identify Ecosystem Services in Changing Landscapes." *Ecology and Society* 18, no. 4.

Markham, A. N. 2018. "Ethnography in the Digital Internet Era: From Fields to Flows, Descriptions to Interventions." In *The Sage Handbook of Qualitative Research,* 5th ed., edited by N. K. Denzin and Y. K. Lincoln. Thousand Oaks, CA: Sage, 650–69.

Markussen, T., and E. Knutz. 2013. "The Poetics of Design Fiction." In Proceedings of the 6th International Conference on Designing Pleasurable Products and Interfaces: ACM, 231–40.

Martin, J., and G. Sneegas. 2020. "Critical Worldbuilding: Toward a Geographical Engagement with Imagined Worlds." *Literary Geographies* 6, no. 1: 15–23. https://www.researchgate.net/publication/342170962_Critical_Worldbuilding_Toward_a_Geographical_Engagement_with_Imagined_Worlds

Mayger, J., L. Liu, Y. Liu, L. Zhu, and Y. Zhao. 2021. "China's Ghost Cities Are Finally Stirring to Life After Years of Empty Streets." Bloomberg Businessweek. September 1, 2021. https://www.bloomberg.com/news/features/2021-09-01/chinese-ghost-cities-2021-binhai-zhengdong-new-districts-fill-up.

McClinktock, P. 2018. "Box Office: 'Black Panther' Becomes Top-Grossing Superhero Film of All Time in U.S." *The Hollywood Reporter,* March 24, 2018. https://www.hollywoodreporter.com/movies/movie-news/box-office-black -panther-becomes-top-grossing-superhero-film-all-time-us-1097101.

McDowell, A. 2019. "Storytelling Shapes the Future." *Journal of Futures Studies* 23, no. 3: 105–12.

McElroy, E., and A. Werth. 2019. "Deracinated Disposessions: On the Foreclosures of 'Gentrification' in Oakland, CA." *Antipode* 51, no. 3: 878–98.

McGrath, J. M. 2020. "The Real Reason Sidewalk Labs Failed in Toronto." TVO. https://www.tvo.org/article/the-real-reason-sidewalk-labs-failed-in-toronto.

McPhearson T, D. M. Iwaniec, and X. Bai. 2017. "Positive Visions for Guiding Urban Transformations Toward Sustainable Futures." *Current Opinion Environmental Sustainability* 22:33–40.

Mead, M. 2005. *The World Ahead: An Anthropologist Anticipates the Future,* edited by R. Textor. New York: Berghahn Books.

Meadows, M., and M. Kouw. 2017. "Future-Making: Inclusive Design and Smart Cities." *Interactions* 24, no. 2: 52–56.

Medeiros E., and A. van der Zwet. 2020. "Sustainable and Integrated Urban Planning and Governance in Metropolitan and Medium-Sized Cities." *Sustainability* 12, no. 15: 5976. https://doi.org/10.3390/su12155976.

Mehdipanah, R., G. Marra, G. Melis, and E. Gelormino. 2017. "Urban Renewal, Gentrification and Health Equity: A Realist Perspective." *European Journal of Public Health* 28, no. 2: 243–48. https://doi.org/10.1093/eurpub/ckx202.

Merrie, A. P. Keys, M. Metian, and H. Österblom. 2017. "Radical Ocean Futures-Scenario Development Using Science Fiction Prototyping." *Futures* 95: 22–23.

Miller, M. J. 2018. "If I Built the World, Imagine That: Reflecting on World Building Practices in Black Los Angeles." In "Race and Spatial Imaginary: Planning Otherwise," edited by L. Bates. *Planning Theory and Practice* 19, no. 2: 254–88. DOI:10.1080/14649357.2018.1456816.

Miller, R. 2018. *Transforming the Future: Anticipation in the 21st Century.* London: Routledge.

Milman, A., and A. Short. 2008. "Incorporating Resilience Into Sustainability Indicators: An Example for the Urban Water Sector." *Global Environmental Change* 18: 758–67. https://doi.org/10.1016/j.gloenvcha.2008.08.002.

Mingye, L. 2017. "Evolution of Chinese Ghost Cities." *China Perspectives* 1: 69–78. http://journals.openedition.org/chinaperspectives/7209

Ministry of Energy. 2015. "UAE State of Energy Report 2015": 5.

———. 2017. "UAE State of Energy Report 2017": 66.

Ministry of Energy and Infrastructure. 2018. "MOEI and EWS-WWF Release List of Top Ten Policy Priorities for UAE to Achieve Its 2050 Renewable Energy Target." UAE. June 3, 2018. https://www.moei.gov.ae/en/media-centre/news /3/6/2018/إطلاق-قائمة-تقرير-سياسة-الطاقة-المستجدة-ووزارة-الطاقة-والصناعة-في-شراكة-مع-جمعية-الإمارات-لحياة-الفطرية.aspx#page=1.

———. 2018. "UAE National Energy Strategy 2050: Presentation for CEM Long Term Energy Scenarios." UAE. https://www.irena.org /-/media/Files/IRENA/Agency/Webinars/UAE-Presentation_LTES .pdf?la=en&hash=7AB6DF56E17BE7CE5841CF5015DA9BE55F10C919.

Minter, A. 2016. "The Burning Truth Behind an E-Waste Dump in Africa." *Smithsonian Magazine,* January 13, 2016. https://www.smithsonianmag.com /science-nature/burning-truth-behind-e-waste-dump-africa-180957597.

Mock, B. 2018. "Wakanda: The Chocolatest City." *Bloomberg CityLab.* February 16, 2018. https://www.bloomberg.com/news/articles/2018-02-16/wakanda -the-prototype-chocolate-city.

Mollenkopf, J. H. 1983. *The Contested City.* Princeton, NJ: Princeton University Press.

Monno, V., and A. Khakee. 2012. "Tokenism or Political Activism? Some Reflections on Participatory Planning." *International Planning Studies* 17, no. 1: 85–101.

Moore, R. 2010. "Roadmap 2050 by Rem Koolhaas's OMA." *Guardian,* May 9, 2010. https://www.theguardian.com/artanddesign/2010/may/09/roadmap -2050-eneropa-rem-koolhaas.

Mumford, L. 1965. "Utopia, the City and the Machine." *Daedalus 94,* no. 2: 271–92. http://www.jstor.org/stable/20026910.

Mzezewa, T. 2021. "Go Ahead. Fantasize." *New York Times,* January 16, 2021. https://www.nytimes.com/2021/01/16/style/go-ahead-fantasize.html.

Nagele, L., D. Wilde, and M. Ryoppy. 2018. "PDFi: Participatory Design Fiction with Vulnerable Users." In *Proceedings of the Nordic Forum for Human-Computer Interaction (HCI) Research,* September 29–October 3, 2018: ACM.

Nandy, A. 1996. "Bearing Witness to the Future." *Futures 28,* no. 6–7: 636–39.

Nared, J., and D. Bole, eds. 2020. *Participatory Research and Planning in Practice.* Cham, Switzerland: Springer.

Natrasony, S., and D. Alexander. 2010. "The Rise of Modernism and the Decline of Place: The Case of Surrey City Centre, Canada." *Planning Perspectives* 20, no. 4: 413–33. http://www-etsav.upc.es/personals/iphs2004/pdf/003_p.pdf.

Nichols, C. (@ChrisNicholasLA). 2018, February 19. "Is there an economy outside of the Wakanda? Are the citizens capitalists? Are the towers residential?

Are they collectively owned? #BlackPanther." Twitter, February 19, 2018, 11:47 a.m. https://twitter.com/ChrisNicholsLA/status/965629034414538752?ref _src=twsrc%5Etfw%7Ctwcamp%5Etweetembed%7Ctwterm%5E96562903 4414538752%7Ctwgr%5E%7Ctwcon%5Es1_&ref_url=https%3A%2F%2F archive.curbed.com%2F2018%2F2%2F19%2F17028794%2Fblack-panther -wakanda-urban-design-architecture-birnin-zana.

Nieto, L., and M. F. Boyer. 2014. *Beyond Inclusion, beyond Empowerment: A Developmental Strategy to Liberate Everyone.* Olympia, WA: Cuetzpalin.

Njoh, A. J. 2010. "Europeans, Modern Urban Planning and the Acculturation of 'Racial Others.' " *Planning Theory 9*, no. 4: 369–78.

Nowosielski, M. 2012. "Challenging Urban Exclusion? Theory and Practice." *Polish Sociological Review* 179, no. 3: 369–83.

Nugent, C. 2020. "The Climate Is Breaking Down. Architect Bjarke Ingels Has a Masterplan for That." *Time,* October 21, 2020. https://time.com/collection /great-reset/5900743/bjarke-ingels-climate-change-architecture.

Nussbaum, M. 2008. "Democratic Citizenship and the Narrative Imagination." *Yearbook of the National Society for the Study of Education* 107, no. 1: 143–57.

Nzinga, A. 2020. "Oakland Residents Skeptical of 'Slow Streets' Project." *Oakland Voices,* April 22, 2020. https://oaklandvoices.us/2020/04/22/ oakland-slow-streets-gentrification-displacement.

Ogilvy, J., I. Nonaka, and N. Konno. 2014. "Toward Narrative Strategy." *World Futures* 70, no. 1: 37–41.

Olah, N. 2014. "The Persian Gulf's 'Blade Runner' Obsession Is Killing Migrant Workers." Vice. May 15, 2014. https://www.vice.com/en/article/8x7k33/the -persian-gulfs-blade-runner-obsession-is-killing-migrant-workers

Oliveira, V., and P. Pinho. "Evaluation in Urban Planning: Advances and Prospects." *Journal of Planning Literature* 12, no. 4: 343–61.

Olson, G. 2015. "Deliberate Dystopias: Uncovering Our Climate Futures with Paolo Bacigalupi." Arizona State University, Global Institute of Sustainability and Innovation, LightWorks, October 14, 2015. https://sustainability -innovation.asu.edu/lightworks/news/archive/deliberate-dystopias -uncovering-our-climate-futures-with-paolo-bacigalupi.

Oteros-Rozas, E., B. Martín-López, T. Daw, E. Bohensky, J. Butler, R. Hill, S. Vilardy et al. 2015. "Participatory Scenario Planning in Place-Based Social-Ecological Research: Insights and Experiences from 23 Case Studies." *Ecology and Society* 20, no. 4: 32.

Ono, R. 2005. "Societal Factors Impacting on Images of the Future of Youth in Japan." *Journal of Futures Studies* 9, no. 4: 61–74.

Osseo-Asare, D. K. 2017. "What a Scrapyard in Ghana Can Teach Us about Innovation." TED Global video, 14:08. https://www.ted.com/talks/dk_osseo_asare _what_a_scrapyard_in_ghana_can_teach_us_about_innovation

———. 2018. Personal communication.

Osseo-Asare, D. K., and Y. Abbas. 2015. "Investigating 3 E-Materials at Agbogbloshie in Accra, Ghana." Paper presented at 2015 Conference on Raising Awareness for the Societal and Environmental Role of Engineering and (Re) Training Engineers for Participatory Design (Engineering4Society), June 18–19, 2015, 41.

———. 2016. "Leveraging Maker Ecosysems to Drive Design-Led Innovation." In *SEED: Innovative Africa.* Zurich: African Innovation Foundation, 5.

———. 2020. "Crafting Space." In *All-Inclusive Engagement in Architecture,* edited by F. Ferdous and B. Bell, 208–16. London: Routledge.

Österblom, H., M. Scheffer, F. Westley, M. van Esso, J. Miller, and J. Bascompte. 2015. "A Message from Magic to Science: Seeing How the Brain Can Be Tricked May Strengthen Our Thinking." *Ecology and Society* 20, no. 4: 16.

Pavlić, E. 2013. "Speechless in San Francisco: Inter-Viewing Films by Barry Jenkins and James Baldwin." *Transition* 110: 102–19. https://www.muse.jhu.edu /article/503535.

Plowman, T. 2003. "Ethnography and Critical Design Practice." In *Design Research: Methods and Perspectives,* edited by B. Laurel, 30–38. Cambridge, MA: MIT Press.

Pierre-Louis, K. 2020. "Wakanda Doesn't Have Suburbs: How Movies Like Black Panther Could Help Us Save the Planet." *Time,* September 21, 2020. https:// time.com/5889324/movies-climate-change.

Polak, F. 1973. *The Image of the Future.* Translated and abridged by E. Boulding. Amsterdam: Elsevier.

Pollastri, S., C. Boyko, R. Cooper, N. Dunn, S. Clune and C. Coulton. 2017. "Envisioning Urban Futures: From Narratives to Composites." *The Design Journal* 20, no. 1: S4365–77.

Potter, C., Osseo-Asare, D. K., and M'Rithaa, M. 2019. "Crafting Spaces between Design and Futures: An Analysis of the Agbogbloshie Makerspace Platform." *Journal of Futures Studies* 23, no. 3: 39–56.

Provoost, M. 2011. Introduction to *Rising in the East: Contemporary New Towns in Asia,* by Rachel Keeton. Amsterdam: SUN Architecture.

———. 2013. "Why Build a New Town?" *Volume,* March 4, 2013. http:// volumeproject.org/2013/03/why-build-a-new-town.

Pruitt, J., and J. Grudin. 2003. "Personas: Practice and Theory." In *Proceedings of the Conference on Designing for User Experiences.* ACM Press, 144–61.

Putnam, R. 1997. "The Prosperous Community: Social Capital and Public Life," *Frontier Issues in Economic Thought* 3: 211–12.

Purcell, M. 2009. "Resisting Neoliberalization: Communicative Planning Or Counter-Hegemonic Movements?" *Planning Theory* 8, no. 2: 140–65.

Raford, N. 2012. "From Design Fiction to Experiential Futures." In *The Future of Futures,* edited by A. Curry. Houston, TX: Association of Professional Futurists.

Ramos, J. 2006. "Consciousness, Culture and the Communication of Foresight." *Futures* 38: 1119–24.

———. 2017. "Linking Foresight and Action: Toward a Futures Action Research." In *The Palgrave International Handbook of Action Research,* edited by L. L. Rowell, C. Bruce, J. Shosh, and J. M. Riel, 823–42. New York: Palgrave Macmillan.

Rangarajan, S. 2018. "Here's the Clearest Picture of Silicon Valley's Diversity Yet: It's Bad. But Some Companies Are Doing Less Bad." *Reveal,* June 25, 2018. https://revealnews.org/article/heres-the-clearest-picture-of-silicon-valleys -diversity-yet.

Rani, R. 2020. "How Covid-19 Inspired Oakland to Get Real about Equitable Urban Planning." *Next City,* October 8, 2020. https://nextcity.org/urbanist -news/how-covid-19-inspired-oakland-to-get-real-about-equitable -urban-planning.

Ratcliffe, J., and E. Krawczyk. 2004. "Imagineering Cities: Creating Liveable Urban Futures in the 21st Century." Dublin Institute of Technology, the Futures Academy. http://www.thefuturesacademy.ie/node/72.

Raven, P. G., and S. Elahi. 2015. "The New Narrative: Applying Narratology to the Shaping of Futures Outputs." *Futures,*14: 49–61.

Rinner, C., and M. Bird. 2009. "Evaluating Community Engagement through Augmentation Maps: A Public Participation GIS Case Study." *Environment and Planning B Planning and Design,* 36, no. 4: 588–601.

Roadmap 2050. 2010. "Roadmap 2050." https://www.roadmap2050.eu/attachments /files/Volume3_FullBook.pdf.

Robinson, K. S. 2020. "The Coronavirus Is Rewriting Our Imaginations." *New Yorker,* May 1, 2020. https://www.newyorker.com/culture/annals-of-inquiry /the-coronavirus-and-our-future.

Romer, P. 2013. "The City as Unit of Analysis." Paul Romer Blog, February 13, 2013. https://paulromer.net/the-city-as-unit-of-analysis.

Rosa, A., and J Sweeney. 2019. "Your Move: Lessons Learned at the Interstices of Design, Games and Futures." *Journal of Futures Studies* 23, no. 4: 137–42.

Rosen, J., M. O'Neill, and M. Hutson. 2018. "The Important Role of Government in Comprehensive Community Initiatives: A Case Study Analysis of the Building Healthy Communities Initiative." *Journal of Planning Education and Research*. https://doi.org/10.1177/0739456X18814296.

Rubin, A. 2013. "Hidden, Inconsistent, and Influential: Images of the Future in Changing Time." *Futures* 45: 38–44.

Rubio, J. M. 2014. "Columbusplein." https://jorgemanesrubio.com/portfolio-item /colombusplein.

———. 2021. Personal communication. July 9. 2021.

Rupini, R. V., and R. Nandagopal. 2015. "A Study on the Influence of Senses and the Effectiveness of Sensory Branding." *African Journal of Psychiatry* 18, no. 2.

Said, E. 1978. *Orientalism.* New York: Random House.

Sandercock, L. 1998. *Towards Cosmopolis: Planning for Multicultural Cities.* London: Wiley.

Schalk, M., T. Kristiansson, and R. Mazé. 2017. *Feminist Futures of Spatial Practice: Materialisms, Activisms, Dialogues, Pedagogies, Projections.* Baunach, Germany: AADR/Spurbuchverlag.

Schiller, J. 2015. "Inside the Hellscape Where Our Computers Go to Die." *Wired,* April 23, 2015. https://www.wired.com/2015/04/kevin-mcelvaney -agbogbloshie.

Schoemaker, P. J. H. 1991. "Choices Involving Uncertain Probabilities: Tests of Generalized Utility Models." *Journal of Economic Behaviour and Organization* 16, no. 3: 295–317.

Schultz, W., and A. Curry. 2009. "Roads Less Travelled: Different Methods, Different Futures." *Journal of Futures Studies* 13, no. 4: 35–60.

Schuyler, D. 2002. Introduction to *From Garden City to Green City: The Legacy of Ebenezer Howard,* edited by K. C. Parsons and D. Schuyler. Baltimore: John Hopkins University Press.

Schwartz, P. 1996. *The Art of the Long View: Planning for the Future in an Uncertain World.* Chichester, UK: John Wiley and Sons.

Schwarz, J. O. 2014. "The Narrative Turn in Developing Foresight: Assessing How Cultural Products Can Assist Organisations in Detecting Trends." *Technological Forecasting and Social Change* 90: 510–13.

Scott, M. 1947. *Western Addition District Redevelopment Study.* San Francisco: San Francisco City Planning Commission.

Seefried, E. 2014. "Steering the Future: The Emergence of 'Western' Futures Research and Its Production of Expertise, 1950s to Early 1970s." *European Journal of Futures Research* 15, no. 29.

Şeker, B. S., and G. Şahin. 2012. "Images of Future Technology Generated By Primary School Students through Their Paintings." *Procedia: Social and Behavioral Sciences* 55:178–86.

Seligman, M., and J. Tierney. 2017. "We Aren't Built to Live in the Moment." *New York Times,* May 19, 2017. https://www.nytimes.com/2017/05/19/opinion /sunday/why-the-future-is-always-on-your-mind.html.

Selin, C. 2006. "Trust and the Illusive Force of Scenarios." *Futures* 38, no. 1: 1–14.

———. 2015. "Merging Art and Design in Foresight: Making Sense of Emerge." *Futures* 70: 24–35.

Sharma, M. 2021. "The Slow Violence of Business as Usual Planning: Racial Injustice in Public Health Crises." Master's thesis, University of Massachusetts, Amherst. https://doi.org/10.7275/20484316. https://scholarworks.umass .edu/masters_theses_2/1023.

Shepard, S., A. Shaw, D. Flanders, S. Burch, A. Wiek, J. Carmichael, J. Robinson, and S. Cohen. 2011. "Future Visioning of Local Climate Change: A Framework for Community Engagement and Planning with Scenarios and Visualization." *Futures* 43, no. 4: 400–12.

Shepard, W. 2015. *Ghost Cities of China: The Story of Cities without People in the World's Most Populated Country.* London: Bloomsbury.

———. 2016. "One Way that China Populates Its Ghost Cities." *Forbes,* January 19, 2016. https://www.forbes.com/sites/wadeshepard/2016/01/19/one-way-that -china-populates-its-ghost-cities/?sh=41c34d6e6e53.

Shipley, R., B. Hall, R. Feick, and R. Earley. 2004. "Evaluating Municipal Visioning." *Planning Practice and Research* 19, no. 2: 193–207.

Slaughter, R. A. 1996. "How to Develop a Social Foresight Capacity." In *Futurevision: Ideas, Insights, and Strategies,* edited by H. F. Didsbury Jr., 88–100. Bethesda, MD: World Future Society.

———. 1998. "Futures Beyond Dystopia." *Futures* 30, no. 10: 993–1002.

———. 2008. "What Difference Does 'Integral' Make?" *Futures* 40: 120–37.

———. 2018. "Two Fine Additions to the Futures Literature." *Foresight* 20, no. 4: 443–46.

Smart Cities World. 2021. "Waterfront Toronto Launches Competition to Find Quayside Partner." https://www.smartcitiesworld.net/news/news/waterfront -toronto-launches-competition-to-find-quayside-partner-6201.

Smith, A. D. 2007. *The Architecture of Adrian Smith, SOM: Toward a Sustainable Future.* Melbourne, Australia: Images.

Smith, N. 2005. *The New Urban Frontier: Gentrification and the Revanchist City.* London: Routledge.

Smith, R. C., K. Vangkilde, M. Kjaersgaard, T. Otto, J. Halse, and T. Binder, eds. 2016. *Design Anthropological Futures*. London: Bloomsbury.

Smith, R. W. 1973. "A Theoretical Basis for Participatory Planning." *Policy Sciences* 4: 275–95. https://doi.org/10.1007/BF01435125.

Social Design for Wicked Problems, 2014. "#1 Amsterdam – West." https://socialdesignforwickedproblems.hetnieuweinstituut.nl/index.html%3Fp=232.html.

Somerville, K. 2009. "The Key Drivers of Organizational Culture Change in the Public Sector: An Analysis of the Canadian Federal Government." Ottawa, Ontario: Library and Archives Canada.

Sönmez, S. Y. Apostopoulos, D. Tran, and S. Rentrope. 2011. "Human Rights and Health Disparities for Migrant Workers in the UAE." *Health and Human Rights* 13, no. 2: 17–35. www.jstor.org/stable/healhumarigh.13.2.17.

Sools, A., and J. Mooren. 2012. "Towards Narrative Futuring in Psychology: Becoming Resilient by Imagining the Future." *Graduate Journal of Social Science* 9:2. http://www.gjss.org/sites/default/files/issues/chapters/papers/Journal-09-02--10-Sools-Mooren.pdf.

Spector, D. 2013. " 'Blade Runner' or Beijing?" *Insider,* January 23, 2013. https://www.businessinsider.com/beijing-smog-and-blade-runner-photos-2013-1.

Srubar, W. 2021. "Engineered Living Materials: Taxonomies and Emerging Trends." *Trends in Biotechnology* 39, no. 6:574–83.

Superflux. 2017. "Future Energy Lab." Superflux website. https://superflux.in/index.php/work/futureenergylab/#. https://courses.ideate.cmu.edu/15-104/f2017/2017/09/01/manuelr-lookingoutwards1-the-future-energy-lab.

Stern, M. 2014. "Measure the Outcomes of Creative Placemaking." In *Proceedings of the Creative Placemaking Conference.* http://www.goethe.de/ins/us/was/pro/creative_placemaking/2014_Symposium_Report.pdf.

Stewart, J., and S. Lithgow. 2015. "Problems and Prospects in Community Engagement in Urban Planning and Decision-Making: Three Case Studies from the Australian Capital Territory." *Policy Studies* 36, no. 1: 18–34.

Streeby, S., N. Hopkinson, C. Fan, and N. Atanosoki. 2019. "Speculative Futures." Proposal to University of California Research Initiatives (UCRI). https://app.dimensions.ai/details/grant/grant.7925754.

Stults, M., and L. Larsen. 2018. "Tackling Uncertainty in US Local Climate Adaptation Planning." *Journal of Planning Education and Research.* https://doi.org/10.1177/0739456X18769134.

Swart, R., R. Raskin, and J. Robinson. 2004. "The Problem of the Future: Sustainability Science and Scenario Analysis." *Global Environmental Change Part A* 14, no. 2: 137–46.

Swim, J., S. Clayton, R. Doherty, R. Gifford, G. Howard, J. Reser, P. Stern, and E. Weber. 2011. "Psychology and Global Climate Change: Addressing a Multi-Faceted Phenomenon and Set of Challenges." American Psychological Association's Task Force on the Interface Between Psychology and Global Climate Change. https://www.apa.org/science/about/publications/climate-change.

Tannenbaum, M. B., J. Hepler, R. S. Zimmerman, L. Saul, S. Jacobs, K. Wilson, and D. Albarracín. 2015. "Appealing to Fear: A Meta-Analysis of Fear Appeal Effectiveness and Theories." *Psychological Bulletin* 141, no. 6: 1178–204. https://www.apa.org/pubs/journals/releases/bul-a0039729.pdf

Tappe, A., and D. Madhok. 2021. "Evergrande and These Chinese Real Estate Developers Are Already in Trouble." CNN Business, October 26, 2021.

Taylor, B. 2020. "How 'Urban Renewal' Decimated the Fillmore District, and Took Jazz with It." KQED, June 25, 2020. https://www.kqed.org/news/11825401/how-urban-renewal-decimated-the-fillmore-district-and-took-jazz-with-it.

Taylor, M. 2007. "Community Participation in the Real World. Opportunities and Pitfalls in New Governance Spaces." *Urban Studies* 44, no. 2: 297–317.

Tellote, J. P. 2014. "Science Fiction Reflects Our Anxieties." *New York Times,* July 30, 2014. https://www.nytimes.com/roomfordebate/2014/07/29/will-fiction-influence-how-we-react-to-climate-change/science-fiction-reflects-our-anxieties.

Textor, R. B. 1995. "The Ethnographic Futures Research Method: An Application to Thailand." *Futures* 27, no. 4: 461–71.

———. 2003. "Honoring Excellence in Anticipatory Anthropology." *Futures* 35: 521–27.

Tharp, B. M., and S. M. Tharp. 2019. *Discursive Design: Critical, Speculative, and Alternative Things.* Cambridge, MA: MIT Press.

Throgmorton, J. A. 1992. "Planning as Persuasive Storytelling about the Future." *Journal of Planning Education and Research* 12, no. 1: 17–31.

Thompson, W. 2016. "How Urban Renewal Tried to Rebuild the Fillmore." Hoodline, January 10, 2016. https://hoodline.com/2016/01/how-urban-renewal-tried-to-rebuild-the-fillmore.

Timmerman, T. 2000. "Survey Design and Multiple Regression: Frequently Encountered, but Infrequently Covered." *Teaching of Psychology* 27, no. 3: 201–3.

Toderian, B. (@BrentToderian) "No cars, walkable streets, super-efficient public transit, place-basedd &culturally sensitive architecture & design at all scales, and & I presume no homelessness or poverty — last night's outing to see #BlackPanther had me wanting to meet #Wakanda's chief city planner."

Twitter, February 25, 2018, 11:10 a.m. https://twitter.com/BrentToderian/status /967793989897220096.

Tschakert, P., and K. A. Dietrich. 2010. "Anticipatory Learning for Climate Change Adaptation and Resilience." *Ecology and Society* 15, no. 2.

Tsekouras, P. 2022. "Two Developers Picked to Build Quayside Neighbourhood on Toronto's Waterfront." CTV News, February 16, 2022. https://toronto .ctvnews.ca/two-developers-picked-to-build-quayside-neighbourhood-on -toronto-s-waterfront-1.5784143.

UAE. 2017. National Energy Strategy 2050. https://www.irena.org/-/media/Files /IRENA/Agency/Webinars/UAE-Presentation_LTES.pdf?la=en&hash =7AB6DF56E17BE7CE5841CF5015DA9BE55F10C919.

UN. 2018. "68% of the World Population Projected to Live in Urban Areas by 2050." https://www.un.org/development/desa/en/news/population/2018 -revision-of-world-urbanization-prospects.html.

UNFCCC. 2022. "Report of the Conference of the Parties Serving as the Meeting of the Parties to the Paris Agreement on Its Third Session, Held in Glasgow from 31 October to 13 November 2021." March 8, 2022. https://unfccc.int /documents.

USGS. 2016. "How Would Sea Level Change If All Glaciers Melted?" Climate and Land Use Change. https://www.usgs.gov/faqs/how-would-sea-level-change -if-all-glaciers-melted?qt-news_science_products=3#qt-news_science _products.

Vaidyanathan, G. 2015. "Big Gap between What Scientists Say and Americans Think about Climate Change," *Scientific American,* January 30, 2015.

———. 2018. "Science and Culture: Imagining a Climate-Change Future, without the Dystopia." *PNAS* 115, no. 51: 12832–35. https://doi.org/10.1073 /pnas.1819792116

van der Heijden, K. 1996. *Scenarios: The Art of Strategic Conversation.* Chichester, UK: John Wiley and Sons.

Van Deusen, R. 2002. "Public Space Design as Class Warfare: Urban Design, the Right to the City, and the Production of Clinton Square, Syracuse, NY." *GeoJournal,* 58, no. 2: 149–58.

van Notten, P. 2005. "Scenario Development: A Typology of Approaches." In *Think Scenarios, ReThink Education.* Paris: OECD Publishing.

van Notten, P. W. F., J. Rotmans, M. van Asselt, and D. Rothman. 2003. "An Updated Scenario Typology." *Futures* 35, no. 5: 423–43.

Vereoort, J., and A. Gupta. 2018. "Anticipating Climate Futures in a 1.5°C Era: The Link Between Foresight and Governance." *Environmental Sustainability* 31:104–11.

Von Hoffman, A. *Why They Built Pruitt-Igoe.* http://www.soc.iastate.edu/sapp /PruittIgoe.html. https://www.worldcat.org/title/why-they-built-pruitt-igoe /oclc/35329586.

Von Stackelberg, P. and A. McDowell. 2015. "What in the World? Storyworlds, Science Fiction, and Futures Studies." *Journal of Futures Studies* 20, no. 2: 25–46.

Wallace, A. 2015. "Sci-Fi's Hugo Awards and the Battle for Pop Culture's Soul." *Wired,* October 30, 2015. https://www.wired.com/2015/10/hugo-awards -controversy.

Wallace, C. 2018. "Why 'Black Panther' Is a Defining Moment for Black America." *New York Times,* February 12, 2018. https://www.nytimes.com/2018/02 /12/magazine/why-black-panther-is-a-defining-moment-for-black -america.html.

Walker, A. 2020. "Coronavirus Is Not Fuel for Urbanist Fantasies." *Curbed,* May 20, 2020. https://archive.curbed.com/2020/5/20/21263319/coronavirus-future-city -urban-covid-19.

Walsh, N. 2022. "Toronto's Quayside Is Back with Projects by Adjaye Associates, Alison Brooks, and Henning Larsen. *Archinect News,* February 17, 2022. https://archinect.com/news/article/150299349/toronto-s-quayside-is-back -with-projects-by-adjaye-associates-alison-brooks-and-henning-larsen.

Wamsler, C. 2013. *Cities, Disaster Risk and Adaptation.* London: Routledge.

Wargo, J. and J. Alvarado. 2019. "Making as Worlding: Young Children Composing Change through Speculative Design." *Literacy* 54, no. 2: 13–21. https://doi .org/10.1111/LIT.12209.

Warner, B. 2018. "Treasure in the Most Toxic Place on Earth." Atlas of the Future, May 12, 2018. https://atlasofthefuture.org/project/amp-agbogbloshie -makerspace-platform.

Warren-Rhodes, K. and A. Koenig. 2001. "Escalating Trends in the Urban Metabolism of Hong Kong: 1971–1997." *AMBIO: A Journal of the Human Environment* 30, no. 7: 429–38.

Watkins, C. 2015. *Gold Flame Citrus.* New York: Riverhead Books.

Watson, V. 2009. " 'The Planned City Sweeps the Poor Away . . .': Urban Planning and 21st Century Urbanisation." *Progress in Planning* 72: 151—193.

Ward, M. 2019. "Thoughts on Critics of Critical and Speculative Design at the Intersection of Critical Reflection and Pedagogic Practice." Speculative Edu. https://speculativeedu.eu/critical-about-critical-and-speculative-design/

Weatherby, C., B. Eyler, and R. Burchill. 2019, "UAE Energy Diplomacy: Exporting Renewable Energy to the Global South." Stimson. https://www.stimson.org /wp-content/files/file-attachments/UAE%20Energy%20Diplomacy_0.pdf.

Wheelwright, V. 2009. "Futures for Everyone." *Journal of Futures Studies* 13, no. 4: 91–104.

Whelan-Berry, K. S., and K. A. Somerville. 2010. "Linking Change Drivers and the Organizational Change Process: A Review and Synthesis." *Journal of Change Management* 10, no. 2: 175–93.

White, R. 2014. "Jane Jacobs and the Paradigm Shift: Toronto 1968–1978." In *Contemporary Perspectives on Jane Jacobs: Reassessing the Impacts of an Urban Visionary,* edited by D. Schubert. Surrey, UK: Ashgate Publishing.

Whyte, W. 1980. *The Social Life of Small Urban Spaces.* Washington, DC: The Conservation Foundation.

World Science Fiction Society, 2020. https://en.wikipedia.org/wiki/Hugo_Award _for_Best_Novel#cite_note-Hugo53-9.

Wosk Center for Dialogue. 2020. "Beyond Inclusion: Equity in Public Engagement." https://www.sfu.ca/dialogue/resources/public-participation-and-government-decision-making/beyond-inclusion.html.

Wylie, B. 2017. "Smart Communities Need Smart Governance." *Global and Mail,* December 5, 2017. https://www.theglobeandmail.com/opinion/smart-communities-need-smart-governance/article37218398/

———. 2019. "Sidewalk Toronto: Violating Democracy, Entrenching the Status Quo, Marking Markets of the Commons." Medium. April 19, 2019. https://biancawylie.medium.com/sidewalk-toronto-violating-democracy-entrenching -the-status-quo-making-markets-of-the-commons-8a71404d4809.

Yaszek, L. 2010. "Afrofuturism, Science Fiction, and the History of the Future." *Socialism and Democray* 20, no. 3: 41–60. https://doi.org/10.1080/08854300600950236.

Yazar, M., D. Hestad, D. Mangalagiu, A. K. Saysel, Y. Ma, and T. F. Thornton. 2020. "From Urban Sustainability Transformations to Green Gentrification: Urban Renewal in Gaziosmanpaşa, Istanbul." *Climatic Change* 160, 637–53. k-3.

Yiftachel, O., and M. Huxley. 2000. "Debating Dominance and Relevance: Notes on the 'Communicative Turn' in Planning Theory." *International Journal of Urban and Regional Research* 24, no. 4: 907–13.

Zaidi, L. 2019. "Worldbuilding in Science Fiction, Foresight and Design." *Journal of Futures Studies* 23, no. 4: 15–26.

Zambonini, H. 2020. "Heaven Is Real: Speculative Critical Design as a Tool for Creating Participatory Futures." Dissertation, the Glasgow School of Art. https://www.academia.edu/43316745/Heaven_is_Real_Speculative_Critical _Design_as_a_Tool_for_Creating_Participatory_Futures.

Zapata, M. A. 2007. "Person-Oriented Narratives: Extensions on Scenario Planning for Multicultural and Multivocal Communities." In *Engaging the Future: Forecasts, Scenarios, Plans, and Projects,* edited by L. D. Hopkins and M. A. Zapata, 261–82. Cambridge, MA: Lincoln Land Institute.

Zapata, M. A., and N. Kaza. 2015. "Radical Uncertainty: Scenario Planning for Futures." *Environment and Planning B: Planning and Design,* 42 , no. 4: 754–70.

Zhou, J. 2012. Urban Vitality in Dutch and Chinese New Towns. A Comparative Study between Almere and Tongzhou. CreateSpace Independent Publishing Platform.

Živaljević-Luxor, N., N. Kurtović-Folić, and P. Mitković. 2020. "Role of Built Heritage in 20th Century Planning and Development of Eurocentric Urban Areas." *Facta universitatis-series: Architecture and Civil Engineering 18*, no. 2: 113–29.

Zukin, S. 2009. Naked City: The Death and Life of Authentic Urban Places. Oxford: Oxford University Press, 200–34.

ACKNOWLEDGMENTS

THIS BOOK WAS WRITTEN with the insight, assistance, and encouragement of many. Eric Cesal, Katharine Dion, Genevieve Hoffman, and Aaron Kelley read early drafts and shaped the result through thoughtful feedback and invaluable discussion. Thank you to the artists and designers behind the projects detailed in these pages—it's been a gift to dive deeper into your work. Many shared hours of time to detail stories about their process, Karl Baumann and Jorge Mañes Rubio in particular. Danielle Emmett, Anthony Gannon, Kelsey Gustafson, Karl Kullmann, Christy Chan, and many others provided intellectual inspiration, artistic collaboration, emotional aid, and feedback on everything from conceptual issues to grammatical phrasing. I was able to finish the text thanks to the funding of the Berggruen Institute and USC and am deeply appreciative of their support. Thank you to Gillian Hamel, Jennifer Eastman, and the rest of the team at North Atlantic for helping make this a significantly better book in the process of editing. Most of all, thank you to my family for your continual tolerance, advice, and care throughout the writing process. You sustain me in countless ways, and I'm forever grateful.

PHOTO ACKNOWLEDGMENTS

THE AUTHOR AND PUBLISHERS wish to thank the institutions and individuals who have kindly provided visual material, and/or permission to reproduce it, for use in this book. Every effort has been made to contact copyright holders. However, should there be any that we have not been able to reach, or any inaccurate acknowledgements made, please contact the publishers, and full revisions will be made to any subsequent printings.

NOTES

AUTHOR'S NOTE

1 As political theorist and philosopher Mark Fisher wrote in 2009, "It's easier to imagine the end of the world than the end of capitalism" (Fisher 2009).

INTRODUCTION

1 Rates of climatic shifts and sea-level rise were based on projections of how high oceans might rise if all glaciers and ice caps in the world melted (USGS 2016).
2 R. W. Smith 1973.
3 Yazar et al. 2020.
4 Sools and Mooren 2012.
5 Keck and Sakdapolrak 2013.
6 Fuchs and Thaler 2018.
7 Adger 2006; Milman and Short 2008; Wamsler 2013.
8 UN 2018.

CHAPTER 1

1 Chang's work was a response in part to vacancies in New Orleans caused by Hurricane Katrina. A resident of the city, she wanted to start a community dialogue about what the many vacant buildings in her area could become. When she found local planning meetings to be overly prescriptive, slow, and low on imagination, she took matters into her own hands and printed the stickers that became "I Wish This Was" (Chang 2010).
2 Streeby, Hopkinson, and Fan 2019.
3 Paul Dobraszczyk describes the dynamic beautifully in *Future Cities: Architecture and the Imagination*, writing that "the imagination is both an active agent—a way of constituting something—and also a transformative faculty."
4 Block 2020.
5 Nugent 2020.
6 Wealth would have accrued, in this case, through increased tax revenue.

7 The same study found that "cultural worldview and environmental value had consistent influence on policy support and environmental action, regardless of message framing" (Chu and Yang 2018).

8 Mzezewa 2021.

9 Seligman and Tierney 2017.

10 This definition is based on work by Keck and Sakdapolrak (2013), who state that social resilience is the ability "to tolerate, absorb, cope with and adjust to environmental and social threats of various kinds."

11 Strong institutional capacity, like the ability of a government to handle complex issues and take care of its citizens, and social ties, such as connections and trust between citizens and existing institutions) together make the building blocks of social resilience (Burton 2015; Folke et al. 2010; Adger 2006).

12 Maclean, Cuthill, and Ross 2014.

13 Nussbaum 2008; Tschakert and Dietrich 2010.

14 Developing deeper levels of empathy is critical when working toward common goals, especially goals linked to navigating uncertainty. The IPCC echoed this train of thought in a 2012 report, insisting that shared modes of imagination are vital to helping communities navigate disturbances and shocks over time (IPCC 2012).

15 As Matt Ward, the former head of design at Goldsmiths, wrote in 2019, speculative futures work "jumps into future ideas and works backwards to understand their potential" (Ward 2019).

16 The RAND Corporation is a think tank affiliated with the US Air Force.

17 Sharon Ghamari-Tabrizi detailed Kahn's process in her 2009 book *The Worlds of Herman Kahn*.

18 Dunne and Raby 2007.

19 Auger 2013.

20 Bruce Sterling first used the term *design fiction* in 2005. Julian Bleecker later built on the idea in 2009 (Lindley 2015).

21 Bleecker 2009.

22 Hales 2013.

23 Bleecker 2009.

24 Hyphen-Labs 2017.

25 According to Hyphen-Labs' description of the effort, it sits at the intersection of product design, virtual reality, and neuroscience, harnessing design fiction to explore deeper conditions of afrofuturistic realities. Afrofuturism as a field is explored in more depth in chapter 7.

26 Candy 2018.

27 Jackson 2019.

28 Worldbuilding is a more ethnographic form of speculative futures (Martin and Sneegas 2020).

29 Schultz and Curry 2009, 37; List 2004.

30 Speculative architect Liam Young distilled the idea in a 2015 interview, insisting that speculative visions that provoke real feeling—love, hate, confusion, and more—helps us to "not just anticipate, but actively shape . . . futures through their effects on collective imagination." For Young, speculation is a means to instigate "debate, raise questions and involve the public as active agents" in how our cities evolve (Duyar and Andreotti 2015).

31 Von Stackelberg and McDowell 2015.

CHAPTER 2

1   Bartels 2017.

2   Bartels 2017.

3   Candy 2020.

4   Levin 2019.

5   Mehdipanah et al. 2017.

6   Mehdipanah et al. 2017; Larsen and Hansen 2008.

7   One of the most extreme proponents of modernism was the architect Le Corbusier. To him, the planner's vision of city space reigned supreme. "A city should be treated by its planner as a blank piece of paper," he wrote, "a clean table-cloth, upon which a single, integrated composition is imposed" (Le Corbusier 1929).

8   Mumford 1965.

9   Much of modernism's allure came from its promise that objective logic would lead to positive social change. Human improvement, according to writer Allan Irving, was seen by the movement's proponents as a simple factor of pushing for "standardized conditions of knowledge and production and a firm faith in the rational ordering of urban space" (Irving 1993, 476; also see Natrasony and Alexander 2010). In this worldview, planning and architectural expertise were guaranteed to benefit society (Provoost 2013).

10 Anti-Eviction Mapping Project 2021.

11 Brahinsky, 2019; Thompson 2016.

12 B. Taylor 2020.

13 The driving force behind redevelopment was the San Francisco Redevelopment Agency (SFRA). It was formed in 1949, not long after President Truman signed the 1949 Housing Act, which authorized the redevelopment of "blighted" neighborhoods. As planner Richard Warren Smith explained in a 1973 paper, the agency's approach was typical of the time, based on the idea that "citizens should be given no power other than the democratic power they already possess; that planning needs to be selective on who it should include; and that participation is valuable because it minimizes confrontation and facilitates the implementation of planning proposals" (R. W. Smith 1973). It was a practice based on the belief that land-use matters were separate from social, economic, and racial issues (Burayaidi 2000), leading to a

kind of minority rule in which experts knew best and everyone else should follow suit. As the movement gained influence, more federal funds were tied to whether cities pushed forward with the urban-renewal approach, regardless of conditions on the ground. Modernist speculative visions developed earlier in the century served as the template that neighborhoods were remade to reflect. The bucolic suburban paradises and orderly urban spaces that modernist architects called for were the idealized speculative futures against which more and more cities were measured.

14 Klein 2008.

15 Klein 2008; Scott 1947, 1.

16 With its predictions of economic growth and cleaner streets, urban renewal had the support of men like Charles Blyth and James Zellerbach, the region's most powerful business tycoons. Through their influence, organizations like the San Francisco Planning and Urban Renewal Association (SPUR) sprang up, providing platforms for corporate interests to shape urban policy, release publications, and actively influence how redevelopment played out across the city. Later, in applications for federal grants to fund work in the Fillmore, planners cited SPUR's input as evidence of the required citizen participation (Mollenkopf 1983; C. Hartman 1984).

17 The work went in two phases. The first transformed sixteen square blocks between 1956 and 1972.

18 After the city bulldozed the area, many lots lay barren for more than thirty years (Klein 2008).

19 Jordan 2016.

20 Ledogar and Fleming 2008.

21 Klein 2008; Fullilove 2004.

22 Across the bay from San Francisco, the school district is seeing a similar, if slower, demise of Black life. Forty years ago, nearly 50 percent of the city's population was Black. Today, those numbers have dwindled by more than half (Levin 2019; Elliott-Cooper, Hubbard, and Lees 2019; Rangarajan 2018; Aldrich and Meyer 2015).

23 Research has shown urban renewal policies have significant impacts on populations that are vulnerable, and those that result in gentrification can result in negative health consequences for the affected populations (Mehdipanah et al. 2017; Elliott-Cooper, Hubbard, and Lees 2019; Rangarajan 2018).

24 Rubio 2014.

25 Bartels 2017.

26 Rubio initially spent significant periods of time with the neighborhood's social workers, meeting with families, learning about the strife that had characterized the area in the past, about programs that had been instituted previously, and those that were still occurring (Rubio 2021).

27 Social Design for Wicked Problems 2014.

28 Beattie, Brown, and Kindon 2020; Coulton, Burnett, and Gradinar 2016.

29 Wargo and Alvarado 2019.

30 A recent paper found that games can effectively reveal "the underlying processes or concepts that drive a system or activity" through the process of play (Coulton, Burnett, and Gradinar 2016).

31 Beattie, Brown, and Kindon 2020.

32 Hansen 2020.

33 Local social workers were invited to translate activities created for the Republic of Columbusplein into daily activities and ongoing initiatives—the idea was to see the area as a source of positive potential rather than a problem to be solved (Eng 2014; Rubio 2021).

34 How to continue coordinating different social concerns in the area, and how to generate and fund new ideas and programs were just some of the logistical questions that contributed to the initiative's eventual fade.

CHAPTER 3

1 Krznaric 2020.

2 The investment was a key part of the UAE's National Energy Strategy 2050 (Jain 2017).

3 Inspirock 2020.

4 Dörrer 2016.

5 Dörrer 2016.

6 Mingye 2017.

7 W. Shepard 2016.

8 Bosker 2018.

9 Bosker 2018.

10 Mayger et al. 2021.

11 Golubiewski 2012; Warren-Rhodes and Koenig 2001.

12 Romer 2013.

13 Cabrera and Najarian 2013.

14 This phenomenon directly contributed to the 2021 demise of one of China's largest real estate developers, Evergrande. The company over-extended its business to the point of threatening default on the substantial debts it incurred to fund China's speculative development craze (Tappe and Madhok 2021).

15 W. Shepard 2015, 2016.

16 Bhattacharya and Sanyal 2011, in Heeyoung 2019.

17 Governa and Sampieri 2019.

18 Provoost 2013; Zhou 2012; Heeyoung 2019.

19 Hardesty 2013.

20 Fu and Zhang 2018; Fu and Zhang 2017.

21 Weatherby, Eyler, and Burchill 2019.

22 Devised in collaboration with the Dubai Electricity and Water Authority, the Future Energy Lab focused on developing research and insights into the energy sector to ensure more a sustainable future for the UAE (Weatherby, Eyler, and Burchill 2019).

23 Superflux 2017; Deck 2019.

24 Zambonini 2020.

25 Superflux 2017.

26 Jain 2017.

27 Jain 2017.

28 Rupini and Nandagopal 2014.

29 UAE National Energy Strategy 2050; UAE Ministry of Energy and Infrastructure 2018.

30 Abdulkarim 2017; Sönmez et al. 2011.

31 Weatherby, Eyler, and Burchill 2019.

32 Li et al. 2020.

33 Li et al. 2020.

34 Abdulkarim 2017; Sönmez et al. 2011.

CHAPTER 4

1 Rem Koolhaas is widely regarded as one of the most significant architects and urbanists of his generation. He won the Pritzker Prize, architecture's most prestigious award, in 2000.

2 Roadmap 2050 2010.

3 Moore 2010.

4 Dunne and Raby 2013; Kahn 1962.

5 H. Hartman 2010.

6 de Graaf 2010.

7 Moore 2010.

8 Kahneman 2011.

9 Holt 2011.

10 Keen 2006.

11 Barber 2013.

12 H. Hartman 2010.

CHAPTER 5

1 Dator 2005; 2019.

2 Selin 2015.

3 Srubar 2021.

4 Eagly and Sczesny 2019.

5 Gebru 2020.

6 B. Crowe et al. 2022.

7 Austen and Wakabayashi 2020.

8 Doctoroff 2016.

9 Fussell 2018.

10 Bliss 2019.

11 Wylie 2017; Wylie 2019; Bliss 2018.

12 Fussell 2018.

13 Hawkins 2019.

14 McGrath 2020.

15 Green 2019b.

16 Haggart and Tusikov 2020.

17 The effort is spearheaded by two firms in particular, Dream Unlimited Corp. and Great Gulf Group (Tsekouras 2022).

18 Walsh 2022; Smart Cities World 2021; C. Crowe 2021.

19 Beginning with questions helps open the mind to what is possible. It enourages asking, "How else might I see this issue?"

20 Modular construction is a toolset and development trend that many architects and researchers believe will become increasingly influential in coming decades (Khubaev, Saakyan, and Makaev 2020).

CHAPTER 6

1 Baumann 2017.

2 Jacobs 1961.

3 Deaken 2007.

4 Klein 2008; Scott 1947.

5 M. P. Brooks 1988.

6 Abd Elrahman and Assad 2021.

7 Harvard University 2022.

8 Zoning barriers, for example, are widely accepted urban principles with Eurocentric origins (Njoh 2010; Živaljević-Luxor, Kurtović-Folić, and Mitković 2020).

9 A 2020 paper led by professor of urban planning Edward Goetz articulated the oversight eloquently, stating that "the focus of planners, scholars, and public discourse on the 'dysfunctions' of communities of color, notably poverty, high levels of segregation, and isolation, diverts attention from the structural systems that produce and reproduce the advantages of affluent and White neighborhoods" (Goetz, Williams, and Damiano 2020).

10 Orisanmi Burton put the situation evenly more bluntly, stating that planning and public safety structures are designed "to protect and serve whiteness" (Burton 2015).

11 Day and the Supreme Court of the United States 1917 (Buchanan v. Warley, 245 U.S. 60).

12 Hernandez 2009.

13 Pavlić 2013.
14 Nieto and Boyer 2014.
15 Lane, Morello-Frosch, Marshall, and Apte 2022.
16 Directory of African American Architects 2021: Data USA 2021.
17 Kimmelman 2021.
18 Bless 2021.
19 City of Oakland 2020.
20 City of Oakland 2021.
21 Fermoso 2020 (minor changes to punctuation).
22 Nzinga 2020.
23 Walker 2020. Also see de Monchaux 2020.
24 Rani 2020.
25 Nzinga 2020.
26 Rani 2020.
27 City of Oakland 2020.
28 LA2050 2016; Baumann 2021.
29 LA2050 2016.
30 Miller 2018.
31 Bates 2018.
32 The team has also continued to share their visions beyond the neighbor-hood, screening the film as an educational example for community organiz-ing in places like the South Side of Chicago (Baumann et al. 2017).
33 Gentrification is still a real threat for Leimert Park, with plans for new residential, commercial, and transit development in the works. For some critics, the workshops have yet to enact enough physical impact on how the neighborhood is changing (Baumann 2021).
34 Baumann 2021.
35 Miller 2018.

CHAPTER 7

1 Watkins 2015.
2 Kunstler 2008.
3 A. D. Smith 2007.
4 Bates 2018; Schuyler 2002.
5 Mumford 1965, 29.
6 The back-and-forth of life imitating art and art imitating life is an ancient dance. The Tower of Babel, a biblical myth explaining why people speak different languages, has been a reference point for people's ideas of cities for eons. Bruegel the Elder painted his famous version of the tower in the sixteenth century. Composer Anton Rubinstein based an entire opera around it in the nineteenth century. The film *Metropolis* depicts elites living

decadent lifestyles in high towers. The more recent film *High-Rise* visualizes social demise by organizing social classes according to their placement in a high-rise building. The reality in many present-day cities like Beijing and Tokyo, where wealthy residents live in tall towers while the poor who serve them exist on the lower floors, is a modern real-life reflection of the Tower of Babel tale (Olah 2014).

7   Haridy 2018.

8   Haridy 2018; H. Jacobs 2018.

9   Ridley Scott's translation of Asian architecture in *Blade Runner* has echoes of Orientalism—the stereotyped ways in which Eastern cultures have been depicted by Western artists, often emphasizing exotification and difference. It's a practice many scholars tie to colonialism, resulting in portrayals that often perpetuate imperialist agendas. Rendering non-Western cultures as exotic and somewhat subservient can help to shore up Westernized concepts of viability and power (Said 1978).

10   Spector 2013.

11   Carmichael 2016.

12   Gold 2001.

13   Kirtley 2014.

14   Lepore 2017.

15   Macdonald 2020.

16   Buxton 2017.

17   Olson 2015.

18   In a recent *New York Times* article, J. P. Telotte, a professor of film and media studies at the Georgia Institute of Technology, wrote that "science fiction does not detail the realities of specific problems so that we might avoid them, but rather represent our most pressing cultural fears" (Telotte 2014).

19   Albarracín 2021; also see Tannenbaum et al. 2015.

20   Earl and Albarracín 2007.

21   Lowe et al. 2006.

22   Vaidyanathan 2018.

23   Vaidyanathan 2018.

24   As Timon McPhearson, director of the Urban Systems Lab at The New School, noted in 2015, "it's difficult to know where you are going if you don't have a clear vision of what that [future] should look like, in particular, a positive vision that you could get excited about and motivated to really make a transformative change" (Vaidyanathan 2018).

25   Writers like Kevin Kelly call this space "protopia" (Kelly 2014).

26   Lee 2020.

27   Gioia 2020.

28   Flatow 2018.

29   Desowitz 2018.

30 As the producer King Britt is quoted saying in a 2014 *Guardian* article, Sun Ra wasn't saying " 'Come with me, I'll save you', but, 'Listen and look at what's around you and we can make this better if you pay attention' " (Bakare 2014).

31 Borchardt 1990.

32 Yaszek 2010.

33 World Science Fiction Society 2020; A. Wallace 2015.

34 According to writer Carvell Wallace, afrofuturism "isn't just the idea that black people will exist in the future, will use technology and science, will travel deep into space. It is the idea that we will have won the future" (C. Wallace 2018).

35 Longtime Leimert Park community members who participated in the workshops, like artist and filmmaker Ben Caldwell, cite afrofuturism as one of their primary inspirations and identities over the decades (Baumann et al. 2017; Baumann 2021).

36 Mock 2018.

37 Visions like Wakanda present essential alternatives to the dominant Western development approach, an approach deeply rooted in colonialism. Cities built today share similar centrally planned and rectilinear notions of space that stem from colonial perspectives (Bates 2018).

38 Toderian 2018.

39 Freemark 2018.

40 Nichols 2018.

41 Corbin's piece goes on to articulate that "the concept art depicts a new Black green urban aesthetic grounded in understandings of African cultural productions; shapes, colors, designs, and functions" (Corbin 2018).

42 Pierre-Louis 2020.

43 Kimmerer 2013.

CHAPTER 8

2 Vereoort and Gupta 2018.

3 As researchers Karen Whelan-Berry and Karen Somerville wrote in 2010, "change initiatives flounder because the ongoing day-to-day business operations take precedence in terms of focus, time and money." Moving beyond the confines of short-term concerns to achieve bigger goals requires identifying "how the change implementation will occur, including how change drivers will be used and when" (Whelan-Berry and Somerville 2010).

4 Armenakis, Harris, and Field 1999; Bridges 2003; Somerville 2009.

5 Adusei et al. 2020.

6 Osseo-Asare 2017.

7 Adjei 2014; Schiller 2015.

8 Minter 2016.

9 One of AMP's cofounders is a native Ghanaian, trained at Harvard University.

10 Osseo-Asare and Abbas 2020.

11 Potter, Osseo-Asare, and M'Rithaa 2019.

12 STEAM is an acronym for science, technology, engineering, arts, and mathematics.

13 Warner 2018.

14 Potter, Osseo-Asare, and M'Rithaa 2019.

15 Potter, Osseo-Asare, and M'Rithaa 2019.

16 Some call this practice of rapidly prototyping the future *futuretyping*.

17 Warner 2018.

18 Adjei 2014; Schiller 2015.

19 Osseo-Asare and Abbas 2020.

20 Dunagan 2018.

21 Integrating speculative futures into planning process is far from a simple fix. Unless fundamental development systems are reformed, speculative futures tools could easily become new forms of virtue signaling. Rather than actually promoting solidary and community reciprocity, they can be co-opted to put creative faces on existing exclusive practices, perpetuating the entrenched inequality, social divisions, and civic tension rapidly increasing today (Hoch 1994; Madanipour 2015).

22 The project was executed with the kind and talented help of Genevieve Hoffman and Anthony Gannon.

23 Wosk Center 2020.

CONCLUSION

1 Gaesser 2013.

2 Von Stackelberg and McDowell 2015.

3 As writer Kim Stanley Robinson declared in the early months of the pandemic, science fiction had become "the realism of our time" (Robinson 2020).

4 As futurist Stuart Candy puts it, "By imagining together in structured ways, and creating the experience of change before it happens, rather than while it's happening, we have a hope of planning [for], and even affecting our future" (Candy 2020).

5 Inayatullah 1998, 815.

6 Bloor 2014.

7 While creating designs to suit all people might sound like a worthwhile effort, doing so can promote the idea that one system should work for all.

8 Macdonald 2021.

INDEX

ABOUT THE AUTHOR

JOHANNA HOFFMAN is an urbanist working in the space between design, planning, fiction, and futures. A founder of the urban futures firm Design for Adaptation, she uses strategic planning and speculative practice to help communities, cities, and organizations survey the impacts of potential futures and spur proactive adaptation. Since gaining an MLA in landscape architecture and environmental planning from UC Berkeley, she has worked for urban design firms on projects around the world. Previously a visiting fellow and researcher at institutions like the Yerba Buena Center for the Arts and the European Futures Observatory, Hoffman is currently a fellow at the University of Southern California. She lives and works in the San Francisco Bay Area.

About North Atlantic Books

North Atlantic Books (NAB) is a 501(c)(3) nonprofit publisher committed to a bold exploration of the relationships between mind, body, spirit, culture, and nature. Founded in 1974, NAB aims to nurture a holistic view of the arts, sciences, humanities, and healing. To make a donation or to learn more about our books, authors, events, and newsletter, please visit www.northatlanticbooks.com.